The PhD Writ

The PhD Writing Handbook

Desmond Thomas

 palgrave

First published 2016 by
PALGRAVE

Palgrave in the UK is an imprint of Macmillan Publishers Limited, registered in England, company number 785998, of 4 Crinan Street, London, N1 9XW.

Palgrave Macmillan in the US is a division of St Martin's Press LLC, 175 Fifth Avenue, New York, NY 10010.

Palgrave is a global imprint of the above companies and is represented throughout the world.

Palgrave® and Macmillan® are registered trademarks in the United States, the United Kingdom, Europe and other countries.

ISBN 978–1–137–49769–7 paperback

This book is printed on paper suitable for recycling and made from fully managed and sustained forest sources. Logging, pulping and manufacturing processes are expected to conform to the environmental regulations of the country of origin.

A catalogue record for this book is available from the British Library.

A catalog record for this book is available from the Library of Congress.

Contents

List of Illustrative Material

► **Tasks**

Acknowledgements

I am deeply indebted to all those who have made a contribution to this book. There are many PhD students at the School of Oriental and African Studies (SOAS) and the University of Essex who have provided me with the examples of their experience and have impressed me with their courage and determination in the face of adversity. Among these, I would like to make specific mention of the following who I have quoted at various points in the book: Wafaa Alfares, Claudia Barrios Alvarez, Georgina Bailey, Evgenia Karetsa, Britanny Kuhn, Andrea Gonzalez Pena, Sujay Prabhat, Melissa Shales, David Sykes.

I am also greatly indebted to my colleague John Trzeciak of the School of Oriental and African Studies for his contribution to Chapter 9, much of which is based on an unpublished article that we wrote together a few years ago.

I would like to thank Mehmet Izbudak, co-teacher of the 'Core Chapter Writing Course' for PhD students that began in 2004 at SOAS and through which many of the ideas contained in this book were first developed. Thanks also to Professor Nadje Al-Ali for giving permission to include the quotation in Chapter 11.

Thanks are due to Richard Lamboll and Valerie Nelson (University of Greenwich) who kindly gave me permission to use an extract from their 2012 'Briefing Paper: Climate Learning for African Agriculture' at http://www.erails.net/FARA/climate-learning. I am similarly indebted to Professor Peter Patrick (University of Essex) for agreeing to the inclusion of an extract from his 1998 paper, 'Caribbean Creoles and the Speech Community', published by the Society for Caribbean Linguistics, St. Lucia.

I would also like to give thanks to Dr Wendy Archer, my co-teacher for many years, who helped design and deliver a year-long 'PhD thesis writing Course' that has provided ongoing support to many PhD student writers at the University of Essex.

Finally, on a more personal level, there are a number of people who I would like to single out for special praise. First, my wife, Liz Austin, for all of her help and encouragement in every aspect of this work. Second, my father-in-law Dennis Austin for his kind words of wisdom. And third, my daughter Adriana Thomas, who is currently engaged in the kind of struggles described in this book as she makes steady progress in her own PhD studies in the Psychology Department at the University of Auckland.

I cannot finish without adding some thoughts on my own experience of PhD thesis writing in the 1990s. In the absence of a guiding handbook such as this one, I turned to my supervisor every time I had a problem related to writing or reading and in particular when I felt I had reached a dead end. I am indebted to Professor Cathie Wallace (University College London, Institute of Education) for all of her wisdom and her clear understanding of the difficulties that I was facing. Without skilled supervisory input, the task of producing a text that does justice to your research becomes that much harder.

I consider myself very fortunate to have been supported by so many people. Thanks to all of you. This book is dedicated to you.

Introduction

A PhD research project presents two types of challenges. The first relates to the project itself, the type of research that is being carried out, its content and its methodology. For these, there are many potential sources of support – individual supervisors, supervisory panels, discipline-related communities and an ever-expanding range of courses and books that offer training and advice on research design, data collection and data analysis.

The other set of challenges relates to the ability to produce a written PhD thesis that will do justice to the quality of your research, enabling readers to understand and appreciate the development of your thinking. This ability will also sustain you throughout a future career in academia, when writing will be the main means of communication with other members of disciplinary and cross-disciplinary communities. It is evident that developing writing skills to the required level will be an important goal for all PhD researchers. However, there is a tendency for writing support to be made available only through occasional self-contained workshops while the need for ongoing support is often underestimated or even ignored.

There are several possible reasons for the relative lack of attention to writing which can characterize research training programmes in higher education institutions. One is the fact that many PhD supervisors and research skills trainers see their responsibilities as limited to giving guidance on content and methods. This is a great pity, as most supervisors and trainers tend to be experienced and skilled writers within their specialist fields. It seems that expertise in writing is rarely passed on from the experienced researcher to the less experienced in an explicit way.

Another reason for the lack of writing support may be an underlying belief that writing is a simple and inherently logical process, which involves working out and clarifying ideas before you write them down. From this perspective, there is a designated order of events where writing comes after reading, collecting data and analysing data as the final stage of PhD research. From this same perspective, writing does not need to be taught. Instead, it is believed that the skills involved can be acquired over a period of time. I have known many cases where PhD researchers were forbidden to write by their supervisors until their third or fourth year of study on the grounds that they might not be ready.

For inexperienced research writers, acquiring the range of skills that they need can present a substantial challenge. The realization that writing a first draft can be a complex and messy process may come very gradually. The stereotype of the inspired writer spontaneously producing a brilliantly clear and coherent text can persist despite strong evidence to suggest that this view of writing rarely matches the reality.

One way of challenging the stereotype is to consider the role of writing and its importance at every stage of the research process. According to Wolcott (1990), writing is not really a product of thinking but is arguably a form of thinking in itself. Putting ideas down on paper or on a screen can be an excellent way of clarifying key issues, helping the writer to see arguments and counterarguments more clearly or examine the strength of the evidence presented to support a particular point that is being made. From this perspective, some form of writing needs to take place even during the very early stages of research, where writing contributes to thinking and helping to make reading more focused.

This handbook seeks to convince you that such an approach to writing can provide a useful basis for developing the skills that you will need to communicate with your intended readers. Some form of writing is present at every stage of the PhD research cycle: this has always been the case and perhaps always will be.

The handbook is divided into sections which follow the process of PhD thesis writing from the initial research proposal up until the final viva.

Chapter 1 considers different models of the PhD and issues related to reading and writing that need to be addressed at the start of PhD research, while *Chapter 2* considers ways of developing a suitable research topic through writing.

Chapters 3, 4 and 5 look at various aspects of reading in order to write: the management of the reading process, issues related to compiling a literature review and the exploration of key concepts.

Chapter 6 considers ways of building a structured chapter framework for the thesis, while *Chapter 7* focuses on the importance of establishing productive writing routines which also include receiving and responding to feedback from various sources.

Chapters 8, 9 and 10 break down the process of first draft writing, examining in turn issues related to clarity and coherence at sentence, paragraph and chapter level, academic style conventions and the drafting and redrafting of text.

Chapter 11 discusses some effective ways of achieving self-motivation and self-discipline in writing, having considered the causes and consequences of writer's block.

Chapters 12 and 13 consider the later stages of thesis writing, including the reporting and analysing of data. Practical guidelines are provided for the effective and systematic editing of written text, the development of oral presentation skills and preparation for the viva.

Finally, *Chapter 14* considers ways in which writing skills can be developed throughout an academic career.

1 The Stages of PhD Thesis Writing

This chapter

- *maps out the different stages of PhD research writing, matching specific writing tasks with the research process for the 'traditional' model of the PhD*
- *compares alternative models such as professional doctorates and 'creative PhDs' and examines the implications for writing in each case*
- *considers the role of the initial research proposal and some of the concerns related to starting writing*

▶ The traditional model of the PhD

The standard or 'traditional' model of the PhD can be considered a kind of academic apprenticeship that emphasizes the production of a written text (a thesis), closely supervised by a specialist in a particular field. In recent years, the emphasis has shifted slightly to take into account the importance of the learning process itself and the acquisition and further development of a range of skills that can be used later in a career.

The stages for the traditional model can be described as below. Note, however, that the sequence will tend to be cyclical rather than linear. For example, reviewing relevant literature will take place in parallel with most of the other activities. Similarly, the initial proposal will be revisited and revised later on.

Developing a research topic and the initial research proposal
This will involve a mix of the following:

- identifying a topic area and clarifying overall aims
- applying feasibility criteria to the area of interest
- breaking down the topic area to give it a clearer focus

- turning this focus into research questions
- generating hypotheses from questions and vice versa (for some research projects)
- identifying and justifying suitable research methods
- building a written rationale around all of the above

Reviewing relevant literature

Reading takes place both before and after the gradual refinement of the research topic. However, once the research questions have been clearly defined, reading can be less exploratory and more focused. Keeping meaningful records of what you have read and the development of your thinking is achieved through notetaking. This means not only summarizing the ideas of other writers but also responding to them via analytical notes. It will be argued that this type of writing is crucial in the early stages of PhD research, since later on the writer will need to reconnect to his/her way of thinking sometimes after a long absence.

Producing a framework for your thesis

Certain unstated expectations of PhD research writing are common to most academic communities. First, there is a requirement to guide the reader through the structure of the thesis itself. The writer is responsible for laying out and developing in a logical fashion the case that is being made, and it is not just up to the reader to make the effort to understand the essence of the argumentation and to plot its development.

Writing draft chapters: general principles and potential problem areas

This will involve a mix of the following:

- identifying readership
- achieving clarity while taking into account style considerations
- achieving coherence: developing and sustaining arguments throughout a chapter
- effective referencing and the provision of substantial evidence to support arguments
- managing the size of the text as it grows
- getting your own position across and making your voice heard
- motivating and disciplining yourself to write

Editing and completing your work

First draft writing and first draft editing will need to be seen as fundamentally different processes. The editing stage of PhD writing has its own set of requirements and specific skill areas. Checklists for editing and for finalizing the text of your PhD thesis can play an important role in achieving success.

At each of these stages, writing is present in one form or another. Table 1.1 gives some examples of typical writing tasks, though they will vary in accordance with the nature of the project. Note that alternative models of the PhD discussed in later sections of this chapter will have different requirements. Wherever this is the case, differences will be clearly highlighted throughout this book.

Table 1.1 Writing at each stage of a PhD research project

	Stage of PhD research project	*Possible writing tasks*
1.	Developing the research topic	• The initial research proposal • An updated written research rationale or revised research proposal • A written application for ethical approval of a research project • Introduction letters and participant consent forms
2.	Reviewing relevant literature	• Summarizing and paraphrasing of key texts • Analytic notetaking in response to key reading texts • Analytic memos or summaries based on the notes • Comparative memos or summaries combining notes from several texts • Annotated bibliographies
3.	Producing a litera-ture review	• Critical reviews of journal articles based on research findings • Literature review draft structure • Exploration and definition of key concepts relevant to the research project
4.	Producing a frame-work for the thesis	• A table of contents and an abstract • A monthly plan
5.	Writing draft chapters	• Chapter overviews • Chapter introductory sections • A reflective writing journal • Reporting of data • Data analysis
6.	Editing chapters	• Editing for content • Editing for structure • Editing for clarity and coherence • Polishing and proofreading

Although some of the tasks included in this table may not seem self-explanatory at this point, each will be considered in greater detail in later chapters of this book. The aim of the overview is to provide an indication of the range of possible writing opportunities at every stage of the research process, not just in the 'writing-up' phase of a PhD.

▶ Alternative models of the PhD

'New Route' PhDs

Many universities now offer 'new route' PhDs as a variant to the traditional model. The aim is to provide a structured programme of formal training to feed into the research project. Students following this route will normally be asked to complete a number of content-related modules along with training in discipline-specific research methods. In some cases, exams will need to be taken and passed in order to be able to upgrade to full PhD level.

The taught element of any 'new route' PhD tends to be front-loaded, with the taught programme of study in the first two years of a four-year cycle. At the time of writing, just over 30 universities in the UK offer this option. However, the number is likely to expand as a more structured research-degree programme appeals to inexperienced researchers who favour a more guided approach to PhD study; this in turn may also provide a wider range of opportunities for writing practice.

The writing requirements for this type of PhD tend not to vary greatly from those of the traditional model. For further details see http://www.newroutephd.ac.uk/.

Professional doctorates

In the last 20 to 30 years, professional doctorates have provided a growing number of practitioners in a variety of fields with the opportunity to upgrade their knowledge and skills. Qualifications such as the EngD (doctorate in engineering) or EdD (doctorate in education) are now widely available as an alternative qualification to the PhD. Meanwhile, fields including medicine, dentistry and psychology offer their own equivalents often linked to registration at a specific level within the profession.

Most professional doctorates include a significant taught or directed study element, which is formally assessed and can involve the accumulation of points or credits up to a required total. In addition, an original piece of research is presented as a doctoral level thesis. The research topic usually relates to an aspect or aspects of professional practice and can be chosen by the researcher, the supervisor or a sponsor. In the latter case, the research is often carried out within a sponsoring institution.

In this type of doctoral programme there are implications for writing which will need to be carefully considered via the following questions:

- Does the directed study element require the production of a portfolio of work in addition to the thesis itself?
- Will the thesis tend to be shorter than in the traditional model? How much shorter?
- How will the two elements be weighted? In some cases, could the importance of the portfolio work outweigh the importance of the thesis?
- Can already published work be included in the portfolio?

Unfortunately, there appear to be no straightforward answers to such questions. Professional doctorates appear to vary greatly in their requirements across institutions and across disciplines. However, taking into account the importance of reflection on professional practice in such programmes, it is advisable to add some extra writing tasks to the list of examples provided for the traditional PhD as detailed in the table below. See also Fulton, Kuit, Sanders and Smith (2013) for further advice in this area.

Table 1.2 Additional writing tasks for professional doctorates

	Stage of research project	Writing tasks
1.	Developing the research topic	Rationale for the research topic: how it relates to issues arising within your practice at a particular point in your career
2.	Writing draft chapters	Personal reflections gained from the research process that are linked to aspects of practice

'Creative' PhDs

Creative PhDs are associated with certain disciplinary areas such as music, film or theatre studies. They combine an original piece of work such as a musical composition, a play or a short novel with an accompanying academic analysis of the creative process, usually referred to as a 'commentary'. Creative PhDs and professional doctorates appear to be similar in some respects, though there is less emphasis here on structured, assessed work.

Box 1.1 gives the reflections of an experienced travel writer, who decided to follow this route towards a PhD. Her task was to produce an original piece of travel writing in the form of a short novel, together with a 40,000-word commentary on the creative writing process:

Box 1.1. One researcher's experience

On the whole, I think it's a very positive experience. You get access to research, sensible and balanced feedback and a framework to ensure that you keep writing (always helpful). Both supervisors and other students are key. However, you are also surrounded by other writers and would-be writers, all of whom have their own, different ideas and will offer masses of helpful suggestions based on what they would do. You will also be reading around your topic. You need to learn and adapt without simply swaying in the breeze towards whichever voice is shouting loudest today. This means keeping a very clear sense of your own identity, vision and voice, and that can be hard to maintain and argue.

For me, coming from a non-academic background, there was also a concern that my writing would be considered too frivolous and that in trying to add enough gravitas to satisfy the academics, I would kill the common touch and make my work unsaleable. Finding that fine balance of depth and readability remains one of my key concerns.

The additional writing tasks involving personal reflections suggested for professional doctorate researchers are likely to be even more applicable for 'Creative' PhDs of this type. An additional problem area which this researcher identifies is the need to communicate in two very distinct styles of writing – one that is appropriate for a travel novel and another which will meet the expectations of an academic readership. Research projects of this type may involve a delicate balancing act to satisfy both types of reader.

PhDs 'by publication' or 'by papers'
An important variant on the traditional model is the PhD 'by publication' or 'by papers'. The original aim of this approach appears to have been to allow a portfolio of already published work to be submitted along with an accompanying piece of analysis that 'typically, critically appraises the submitted works, explains how they fit together, accounts for and supports their chosen methodologies, and highlights the significant and original contribution to scholarship' (Willis and Cowton, 2011).

However, the notion of a 'Publications PhD' seems to have been merged into a more recent variant – the 'PhD by papers' consisting of several pieces of hitherto unpublished work linked together by a common theme. It is therefore possible for researchers who have little or no published work to follow this route. In some cases it is even presented as a less arduous and more focused option.

The fact that a PhD by papers might be presented as an easier option than the traditional model is a cause for concern. PhD supervisors may feel that the benefits will outweigh the drawbacks, taking into consideration the need to have work published in a highly competitive academic environment. However, choosing the 'by papers' model may have some or all of the following consequences:

- a requirement to conduct separate literature reviews for each of the papers included in the thesis
- a requirement to develop and describe separate methodologies for each research paper
- the near inevitability of having to present early attempts at conducting research alongside later, more sophisticated attempts. In this scenario, the researcher will usually develop and present a different paper for each year of the research process
- the difficulty of achieving overall coherence between so many different texts
- a lack of definition relating to the nature of the analytic commentary that aims to bind the thesis together
- the amount of time and effort that can be spent submitting work for publication, and in many cases having to cope with multiple rejections

Despite all of these potential difficulties, many inexperienced researchers find this model of PhD to be very productive. A collection of publishable papers can be highly advantageous for anyone starting an academic career. Other arguments in favour of this model include the following:

- As the papers are peer reviewed, you are able to receive more extensive feedback than is often the case during the production of a traditional PhD thesis.
- Successful publication will give a boost to your self-confidence during the final stages of your research project.
- Successful publication almost acts as a guarantee that you have already reached the required standard.
- In some projects of this type, there are also possibilities for fruitful co-authorship initiatives without risking a loss of overall control.

To obtain a balanced view of the advantages and disadvantages of this model, it is useful to consider the experiences of other researchers:

Box 1.2. One researcher's experience

My supervisor told me that the best option is the paper-based PhD. I'm still not quite certain whether it is the best. I have to do three papers which all need to be linked. I will need to do three different data sets. None of the papers have been published yet. It's the same for other students in my department. He never suggested that I should include my two papers that have already been published in a related area. I need to write two new papers alone and one that is co-authored. That's really good because you can do something with your supervisor or with another person – in my case I am working with another person who helped me with the data.

► Making a start

The initial research proposal

According to one PhD thesis writer, 'When I look at my first proposal, I just laugh. There were about ten PhDs in it. But it still represents a starting point.'

Your very first proposal is often unrealistic and may even constitute your first attempt at writing after a long gap. An initial proposal can be deliberately broad and vaguely worded, because you may be trying to find the right person to supervise your work and do not want to close down your options. However, an initial proposal is still an important document because it is the first point of contact between a researcher and the academic department that will support and guide the research project. In addition, it provides the first opportunity for many PhD researchers to clarify thinking through writing. During the early stages of PhD research, it will be reconsidered and revised until it is transformed into a more focused rationale that will act as a point of reference throughout your project.

Different institutions will offer their own templates for completing an initial proposal. You will normally be required to consider each of the following:

- the broad topic area that you would like to research
- the reasons for choosing this topic and its significance
- research aims and questions
- research methodology

- key references
- your intended research plan

In arts, humanities and social science areas, such a proposal will act as a starting point for your research. In the natural sciences, this may also be the case: however, there will also be situations in which this format is not applicable – for instance, if you are applying to join an existing project led by a principal investigator.

Whatever the circumstances, your initial proposal serves two important functions, which can be summarized as follows:

1. *It helps you to develop your ideas relating to a chosen topic in a structured way.*
   Your first piece of writing also represents your earliest attempt to take control of your topic area and develop it further. It will be an important document to look back on much later in your research and will act as a reference point to show you how far you have progressed.
2. *It demonstrates to your readers your ability to express your ideas clearly, concisely and coherently.*
   An initial proposal is rather like an application to become a member of an academic community, where, it is hoped, you will become a respected researcher and colleague. The impression that you make on your readers must therefore be carefully considered.

Some initial concerns

Starting PhD research can sometimes be an overwhelming experience in which much new information needs to be absorbed, new connections need to be established and expectations need to be carefully adjusted to suit new circumstances. It is important to realize that you are not alone and that others who lack research experience will share your concerns. Here is a selection of comments offered by a group of PhD research students from a range of disciplines at the very beginning of their journey:

Which aspects of a research project concern you most?

- knowing where to start
- putting together a realistic plan that works for me in the timeframe
- not becoming too obsessed and letting the PhD take over my life
- that I won't have a critical standpoint and won't make an original contribution to the field
- time management

- identifying the right research question which I can answer in the time-scale available
- how to make the best use of my supervisor and how to expand my network to gain insights from others
- presenting my work at conferences
- missing the panoramic view in an attempt to complete all of the tasks required of me
- that everyone will know I am a fraud and shouldn't be here

In this book, we will address such general concerns, as well as those which are more directly related to reading and writing, illustrated through the examples below:

Which aspects of research reading and writing concern you most?

- There is no flow in my writing
- I easily feel anxious and overwhelmed by important writing tasks, meaning that I have a tendency to procrastinate dangerously
- I need to learn to read systematically and improve my ability to read effectively
- My approach to reading and writing is too labour-intensive and therefore unsustainable. I need strategies for reading that do not involve reading every word of a book and making detailed notes
- The literature review is very stressful
- I am not producing enough written text due to writer's block, panic or anxiety
- Since I am not a native English speaker, it worries me a lot that my language will affect the quality of my thesis
- Have I done enough reading and writing? Or do I need to do more? How will I know?

Action Points

1. <u>Start some form of writing</u> as early as possible.
2. Draw up <u>a list of writing tasks</u> that will suit the type of PhD that you are engaged in.
3. Use even simple writing tasks to <u>focus your discussion</u> with your supervisor and other intended readers.
4. Write down a list of <u>your expectations</u> at the very beginning of the research writing process. It is essential that you compare your

expectations with those of your intended readers. Find answers to questions such as, 'How much writing am I expected to produce in the first six months of my research project?'

5. Write down a list of your general <u>concerns</u> and those specifically related to research reading and writing. Refer to the sample lists above. Try to <u>categorize</u> these problem areas. Which of them must be discussed immediately and which of them can wait? Talk to peers to compare views.

6. Prepare <u>an initial research proposal</u> (even if this is not required) by following a recommended template. Revise and develop it regularly.

2 Developing a Research Topic through Writing

This chapter

- *considers three basic criteria sets for choosing a suitable research topic*
- *examines ways of breaking down a research topic through writing*
- *explores the relationship between topic development and the successful completion of writing tasks, such as the production of an updated research rationale*

▶ Choosing a topic

There are many possible reasons for the initial choice of a research topic at PhD level. Sometimes the choice may be limited by practical constraints such as supervisor availability. For some, the choice is determined by the supervisor's own interests or by financial incentives such as scholarships or study grants. In joint research projects with a designated principal investigator, individual choice may appear to be limited. But when choice is a real option, the freedom to choose can sometimes become problematic and even burdensome – in particular for those who have spent many years of their lives responding to questions that have been posed by others.

How do researchers make their initial choice of topic and justify this choice? Answers to this question can be surprisingly varied and include the following, where the supervisor's role and influence is a deciding factor:

- *My supervisor suggested some topics and I chose one (computer science).*
- *My supervisor chose this topic for me (computer science).*

- *I am part of a funded project on connections between food production, energy security and climate change. The PhD topic was formulated for me, although it is fairly free for me to interpret (sociology).*
- *This is the research area of my supervisor. It was also a completely new topic for me and I wanted to learn something new (economics).*
- *I chose my supervisor based on a common interest in railways. For the specific topic, I am following my supervisor's advice (computer science).*

Sometimes the reasons are more personal, as in these examples:

- *a question arising from my experience (history)*
- *expanding from my previous research (computer science)*
- *something that grew out of my MA thesis (art history)*
- *based on a personal work experience (business studies)*
- *this topic is a challenge to classic theories whose assumptions I do not like (business studies)*
- *I am not satisfied by the recent literature (history)*
- *there are several blind spots in the historical literature on mandate Palestine (history)*

The initial identification of a topic or topic area is the starting point for a series of activities in which the overall aims of the project and its precise focus are gradually explored, defined and specified through writing. There are, unfortunately, no scientific studies that demonstrate beyond any doubt a clear link between the quality of decision making at this stage and subsequent success. However, there is certainly evidence to suggest that the use of effective strategies in the initial phase of developing the research topic can make a real difference in the long run. See, for example, the views of Blaxter, Hughes and Tight (2001); Brewer (2007); or Wolcott (1990) in this respect.

It is useful to break down the process of topic development into a series of questions that all researchers will need to address:

i.   What criteria need to be taken into consideration when choosing and refining a PhD research topic?
ii. How can a research topic be developed so that its aims and focus are clear?
iii. How can suitable research questions and claims be generated?
iv. How important is a written rationale or revised proposal at this stage?
v.   How can a suitable revised rationale for the research be developed?

These questions will be considered and possible answers explored in the remaining sections of this chapter. In response to the first question, three basic criteria sets for choosing and developing a suitable research topic will be considered:

- *feasibility* (is the topic manageable?)
- *specificity* (is it clearly defined?)
- *significance* (does it contain sufficient elements of originality and is it of interest to a particular community of readers?)

▶ Finding and developing a topic that is feasible

The initial choice of research topic may often seem to be perfectly reasonable, but a closer examination can reveal its flaws. Feasibility criteria can help to determine whether it should remain as an idea on paper or whether it can be put into practice. Although the consideration of feasibility criteria is a relatively straightforward task, there are a still a number of issues to consider here. Clearly, some will have greater prominence than others depending on the type of project being undertaken and the context of the research. It will be seen that some of the criteria are directly linked to specific writing tasks; others less so.

The size or scope of the study proposed

This is where feasibility links closely with specificity. An initial choice of topic may be over-ambitious for many reasons. In itself, this is not entirely disadvantageous, since it is important not to narrow the range of choices too soon. However, there comes a point where a lack of focus can make the project unmanageable.

As Wolcott (1990) and other writers suggest, writing plays an important role in clarifying thinking. It could be argued that nowhere is this more pertinent than at this initial stage of the research process. A linear approach to topic selection and development can result in a dead end, whereas exploring lateral links through a written mapping exercise can often be seen to be more productive. An example of how this might work is presented later in this chapter.

The amount of time and other resources available

Your research project can succeed only if the resources that it needs are freely available. The amount of time involved is clearly a key factor in the planning of any research project. In the UK context, this has become even more important in recent years as completion dates have been strictly enforced. Restricted financial or technical resources can also determine project feasibility.

The range of technical skills needed to carry out the study

If, for example, the success of a project depends on your ability to master a new language or achieve a high level of technical competence in the use of sophisticated equipment, the extra burden that this adds to the workload may render the whole project unfeasible.

Access and availability of data and information

If the research project depends for its success on important data that is locked away, it is obviously necessary to know in advance that the key will be made available. Data can become unavailable in other ways as well, for example if the services of a highly skilled translator with knowledge of a particular subject area is required. Special visas or letters of introduction may also determine whether access is granted to sensitive data to be collected as part of a fieldwork exercise. One essential writing task at this stage may well be the production of a suitably worded letter outlining the aims and benefits of the research and requesting such access.

The level of risk (of various kinds) attached to the project

Risks can be physical, psychological, financial or reputational. You, participants in your research or the participating institutions could be at risk. Certain topics can seem to lend themselves to particular kinds of risk. For example, investigations into 'corrupt practices' may endanger research participants who give honest opinions affecting the reputations of those seen to be involved. Such research needs to be carefully considered to ensure that the benefits clearly outweigh the risks, and a realistic assessment needs to be made of the levels of risk. Risk assessment and ethical considerations (see below) are often inextricably linked.

The website of the UK Social Research Association offers a code of practice to protect the safety of social researchers. This can be found in Appendix 1.

Theoretical basis for the research

A research project may not be feasible if it seeks to fill a perceived gap in knowledge that is seen by other researchers in the field to be difficult to address. Similarly, a project is less likely to be feasible (at least within the constraints of PhD research) if there are no existing theoretical or conceptual frameworks that can help make sense of underlying issues. Another reason for rejecting a project on feasibility grounds would be if it is based on a claim or series of claims for which there is little supporting evidence. Finally, a project that seeks to demonstrate a strong association between two apparently unrelated concepts could be difficult to justify.

Unsurprisingly, writing has an important role in determining feasibility in these areas. To justify conducting research in an area where there is an apparent gap, a strong rationale would be required to demonstrate the feasibility and also the significance of the project. To justify claims which appear to lack supporting evidence, a short literature review would probably need to be presented. To demonstrate the validity of an association of ideas which may seem counterintuitive to other researchers in the field, a preliminary research paper might even be required.

Whether key terms can be clearly defined or not

This may seem an unlikely reason for a research topic to be rejected. However, wherever key terminology resists definition, there is often a good reason. The role of writing here is clear: the concepts and their labels will need thorough exploration leading to definitions which can be considered acceptable within the context of the research.

Whether the phenomena being explored are recent or subject to rapid change

If the aim of your research is to attempt to analyse very recent events or phenomena that are in the process of rapid change, there are potential dangers which need to be carefully considered. If, for instance, a project is likely to produce data that will be superseded by the time of publication, such a consideration may lead to its rejection on feasibility grounds.

Whether the researcher is able to maintain a suitable distance

For very recent events, there is the added problem of achieving distance between an unfolding narrative and your own position. Locating the research within a fixed period in the recent past is one means of addressing this, with the intervening time period separating the two. Even if such 'distancing strategies' are adopted, the close involvement of the researcher in any project needs to be carefully considered, particularly if there is a strong emotional involvement in some of the issues involved. If the research involves advocacy of a particular perspective that is shared by the researcher, this needs to be made explicit. But if objectivity rather than subjectivity and professional distance rather than close involvement are the aims, the feasibility of carrying out the project needs to be carefully considered.

There are significant implications for writing in this area. According to Grbich (2007: 10), in certain types of research projects (for example, those which promote a postmodernist approach) 'reflexive subjectivity replaces objectivity'. She adds: 'Self-reflexivity involves a heightened awareness of the self in the process of knowledge creation, a clarification of how one's beliefs have been socially constructed and how these values are impacting on interaction, data collection and data analysis in the research setting'. This awareness of your own values and their impact would need to be carefully explored in one of the introductory chapters of the thesis itself.

Ethical considerations

The ethics of research is clearly an area of the greatest importance and one which will need to be explored within the context of each individual research project and the related disciplinary areas. Brewer (2007: 71–2) provides a useful explanation of the main ethical issues to be considered within the context of research feasibility, which are summarized below. You will need to ensure that:

- *physical, mental, social or environmental damage of any form does not result from the research. Vulnerable people need to be suitably protected. This could include 'the elderly, children, the mentally ill, the physically handicapped or other disadvantaged people'*
- *participants are informed of the true purpose of the research*
- *participants give their consent to take part willingly and freely*
- *anonymity and confidentiality must be observed if offered to participants*
- *the reputation of participating institutions will not be damaged by the research*

Some of the items on Brewer's list, summarized above, do not seem to be at all contentious. The kind of experiments conducted by psychologists 40 or 50 years ago in which some degree of harm to participants was regarded as a tolerable by-product would no longer be accepted by most research communities. For an illustration of how attitudes have changed, see the replicated experiment reported by Burger (2009).

Other points, however, do raise some interesting questions. An example is the requirement not to cause reputational damage to participant institutions. Does this mean that any criticism of such an institution should cause the project to be considered unfeasible on ethical grounds? There is an apparent contradiction here as research which deliberately sets out to avoid the less attractive characteristics of a sponsoring institution could also quite arguably be considered unethical. Clearly, a balance needs to be achieved between the need to present negative aspects along with positive and the responsibility to prevent unwarranted damage to individuals' or institutions' reputations.

Brewer's summarized list of points might seem to be incomplete to many readers. The following ethical considerations affecting feasibility could justifiably be added:

- constraints imposed by third parties (for example, health and safety regulations)
- conflicts of interest (for example, with research sponsors)
- manipulation of facts and data (for example, selective presentation of findings)

For a useful set of guidelines specific to 'proper scientific conduct in research', see Appendix 1.

An important writing task that will precede data collection is the production of a written proposal to be submitted in order to gain ethical approval for the research project. This is generally a requirement of higher education institutions across all subject areas. The ethical approval application will usually require the following: a short written rationale for the project; an account of how data collection will take place; and a justification for the methods of collection and analysis that will be used.

Task 2.1 shows possible research topics that have been formulated as research questions. Clearly, many of them would <u>not</u> be feasible as they are presented here. Which ones would need to be summarily rejected? On what grounds? Some of the topics, however, might contain the potential for a possible PhD research project. Could any of them be modified so that they would be feasible? What changes would need to be made and why?

Task 2.1: Evaluating sample topics

Topic lists are based on research students' initial expressions of interest, the majority at PhD level. Suggested answers to the questions above are provided in Appendix 2.

1. What are the most successful marketing strategies for airline companies?
2. What is the difference between management styles in Japan, the UK and the USA?
3. What are the most effective strategies for dealing with the latest generation of computer viruses?
4. Is tourism beneficial or harmful to less developed countries?
5. What are the long-term effects of sleep deprivation?
6. What impact is the land reform policy in Zimbabwe having on the local economy?
7. What impact will global warming have on the Maldive Islands?
8. What is the best way to improve the pronunciation of students learning English as a foreign language?
9. Do high levels of creativity lead to psychological disturbance?

Task 2.2: Evaluating your own topic

How could the feasibility of your own proposed research topic be evaluated? Comment on the following, as far as you are able:

a) the size or scope of the study proposed
b) the amount of time and other resources available
c) the range of technical skills needed to carry out the study
d) access and availability of data and information
e) the level of risk (of various kinds) attached to the project
f) whether the project has an adequate theory base and whether implied claims or connections can be sustained
g) whether key terms can be clearly defined or not
h) whether the phenomena being explored are recent or subject to rapid change
i) whether you are able to maintain a suitable distance from the object(s) of research
j) ethical considerations

▶ Finding and developing a topic that is specific and significant

When beginning a new project, many researchers find that their initial choice of topic is far too broad and lacks specificity. This is not necessarily a disadvantage at the very start, since specificity implies a commitment to a particular direction for the research. In other words, one avenue is chosen and a decision is made to leave other possible avenues unexplored. Clearly, there are great dangers in making such choices too soon.

A greater danger, however, lies in maintaining a lack of specificity. In the early stages of a PhD research project, you will need to think about how to work on the topic area so that it begins to resemble the kind of title that you would be happy to see on the cover page of the finished text. An example of an unspecified topic could be the following:

'Educational Change in Post-Communist Societies'

An initial breakdown of this topic area might lead in one or more of these directions:

A particular country:	*Bulgaria*
A specific period of time:	*1989–2000*
A particular field of education:	*Secondary schools*
A particular group of people:	*Secondary school teachers*

Working in <u>linear</u> fashion in any of these directions means that we do not concentrate on any of the others. We can also miss interesting <u>lateral</u> links in the process (see below). However, the starting point for developing a potential topic might still be linear, making use of existing models for topic development.

Booth, Colomb and Williams (1995: 49–51) propose an interesting and innovative structured process for breaking down a research topic, as well as developing different levels of research questions and, ultimately, the research thesis or 'main claim'. The stages that follow are mostly based on their original model, using different stage labels and with illustrative examples added. However, extra stages have been added to their structure to provide a more complete picture of how a research topic might be fully developed and transformed into a draft title.

Stage 1: Defining the broad topic area

At this stage, you will need to find appropriate ways of completing this type of sentence:

'I am studying ...' 'I am interested in exploring ...'

Box 2.1. Stage 1 examples

1. *I am studying Nepal's political culture and the idea of Hindu kingship*
   This topic might be a good starting point for a piece of research, but it is one which clearly needs to become more focused.
2. *I am interested in exploring the political agendas of various European governments in the mid nineteenth century and the development of the transport system in Brazil.*
   This topic already has a narrower focus, but there is still room for further refinements and modifications. Which European governments are of most interest? Which aspects of the transport system merit closest study?

Stage 2: Generating specific questions in a detailed breakdown

This stage consists of questioning the topic area in different ways, making the aim and focus of the research more clearly defined, as below:

'I am interested in exploring ... because I particularly want to discuss ...'

Box 2.2. Stage 2 examples

1. *I am studying Nepal's political culture and the idea of Hindu kingship because I want to explore the role of the king in Nepalese society OR ... because I'm interested in possible changes in this role since 1900.*
2. *I am interested in exploring the political agendas of various European governments in the mid nineteenth century and the development of the transport system in Brazil because I want to find out the extent to which various governments at the time were interested in the development of Brazil as a nation.*

   OR ... because I want to know why there was so little interest in developing the railway system, compared to the situation in other countries in the region.

Moving from stage 1 to stage 2 seems relatively straightforward, but there is a danger that the topic will quickly become channelled into one or two very specific questions, when there is the possibility of addressing other questions that may turn out to be more significant. For this reason, it is a good idea to try to generate a wide range of such questions around the topic and to question each element of the topic when it is broken down into parts.

Box 2.3. A simple way of breaking down your own research topic in detail

Producing a mind map or another type of organizational diagram is one way to identify sub-topics that may lead the research in interesting directions. The diagram can be tailored to both your needs and your preferences. Here is an example of one type of diagram:

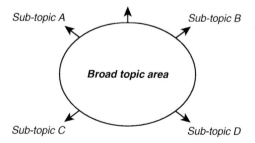

Each sub-topic can lead the research in a different direction and can be broken down further. Interesting **lateral links** may also appear across sub-topics, leading to the emergence of unexpected new research questions.

Practise generating as many questions as you can, based on this type of 'mind map' for your own research topic. Can you suggest examples of more complex questions that emerge when different sub-topic areas are linked together?

An example of how this might work is provided in Fig 2.1:

Bulgaria
Educational
Change

Fig 2.1 Breaking down a research topic

Possible directions for the arrows might include the following considerations:

- socialism/communism influences
- pre-World War 2 traditions
- post-1989 influences
- change vs reform
- different perceptions of change
- different perceptions of reform
- consequences of change
- different educational sectors

Here are some possible research questions that could emerge from this example, either taking the research in one of the specified directions or combining more than one of them by moving in a lateral direction.

1. What have been the attitudes of Bulgarian post-communist governments towards educational reform?
2. To what extent is educational reform seen as a reaction to socialism/communism?
3. To what extent have pre-World War 2 educational traditions been reintroduced?

Task 2.3: Break down your own research topic using the diagram below:

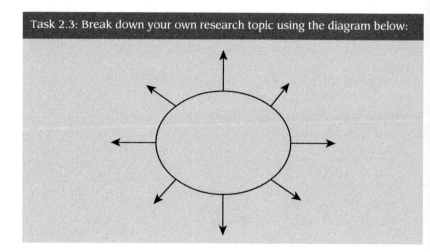

Now produce as many questions as you can for your own topic by using the map above. If questions seem rather simplistic, this does not need to be an immediate cause for concern: they can be combined into more complex questions later, making use of lateral connections that may become apparent as different directions are explored.

Stage 3: Finding significant research questions

So far in this chapter, three basic criteria sets for choosing a suitable research topic have been proposed, namely *feasibility* (is the topic manageable?), *specificity* (is the topic clearly defined?) and *significance* (is the topic of interest to a particular academic readership?). In this section, we examine the third of these.

At this point, the problematic concept of 'originality' also needs to be considered. Murray (2002) and other writers argue that this is perhaps the 'key criterion for doctoral work.' At the same time, there are so many possible interpretations of what might constitute original work that the concept appears to be elusive and to resist a clear definition.

Phillips and Pugh (2005) provide a range of definitions apart from that of 'setting down a major piece of new information in writing for the first time'. These include:

i.   carrying out empirical work that has not been done before
ii. using familiar material but adding new interpretations
iii. conducting familiar research but in a different context
iv. bringing new evidence to bear on previously debated issues

In other words, it is not necessary for a doctoral research project to break completely new ground as the 'original' label might suggest. Taking small accumulative steps which add to the existing store of knowledge in a specific field will suffice. For this process, the term 'significance' will be preferred throughout this handbook as a more meaningful alternative. Thus, rather than asking 'is the topic original?', the question 'is the topic of interest to a particular academic readership and therefore significant?' will be seen to provide a more appropriate reference point.

What makes a particular research question one that has real significance for readers in a particular field? This can be a difficult question to answer immediately. At some point, the following sentence will need to be completed:

'I am interested in exploring ... X ... in order to help readers understand ...'

Box 2.4. Stage 3 examples

1. *I am studying Nepal's political culture and the idea of Hindu kingship and am interested in possible changes in this role since 1900*

   - *in order to help readers understand the historical reasons for the progressive erosion of political consensus in Nepalese society since 1995.*
2. *I am interested in exploring the political agendas of various European governments in the mid nineteenth century and the development of the transport system in Brazil*

   - *in order to help readers understand that there may have been a direct link between interventions made by successive British governments and the quality of the transportation network in Brazil today.*

Moving from stage 1 to 2 helps focus your research, narrowing the topic area. Moving from stage 2 to 3 implies addressing a *research problem* that is significant to a community of readers. While it is likely that the nature of this problem (or underlying question) will not be clear at the beginning of the research, you can be confident that it will become clear eventually.

There are various ways of finding a suitable research problem in a particular field of enquiry:

- talking to others, taking part in discussions and debates
- presenting your research in a structured oral presentation, followed by a question-and-answer session
- reading – detecting contradictions, inconsistencies or incomplete explanations
- brainstorming the topic and generating multiple questions, especially when new connections are established

For cross-disciplinary research topics, this process becomes even more important as each field of inquiry may approach key issues underlying your research in a slightly different way.

Stage 4: Adding research questions linked to practical applications
Most researchers will be able to skip this stage entirely. However, some research projects, in addition to having significance for a particular community, will go beyond the issues under discussion in order to arrive at practical applications or solutions to specific problems. This may be the case, for instance, if you are working towards a professional doctorate and there is an expectation that your thesis will provide recommendations based on your research findings that will involve a reappraisal of current practices in your field. This sentence then requires completion:

'I also want readers to be able to consider ways of ...'

Box 2.5. Stage 4 examples

1. *Restoring the political consensus in Nepal.*
2. *Solving Brazil's current transport problems.*

There are obviously great dangers inherent in 'jumping to solutions' before the nature of the actual problems has been fully explored. In many cases, considering practical applications will prove a step too far. At worst, consideration of practical outcomes or benefits of the research can prove a major distraction.

Stage 5: Turning a research problem into a claim or hypothesis
Once a research problem has been identified, the next step might be to clarify the *main claim or thesis* that will underpin the chapters that you

will produce. Many social science disciplinary areas favour this kind of approach, however others make it clear that they do not. In some cases, the formulation of specific hypotheses that can be tested against the data may be compulsory. At the other extreme, some disciplines require the exact opposite, stipulating that all hypotheses or claims should emerge from empirical data. It is important to clarify from the outset which of these approaches you will need to adopt. If stage 5 is relevant to your own research project, the following questions (in italics) will need to be asked.

What kind of claim will you make?

Having presented the problem in the form of the key question or questions to be addressed, you then need to consider how you think these questions could and should be answered. These answers will provide you with a central hypothesis or main claim and will establish your own stance vis-à-vis the research problem.

Will your readers accept its significance?

This is much harder to determine and will depend on the level of your claim and the expectations of readers in your particular area. Booth, Colomb and Williams (1995) point out that in some fields of research, it is enough to present new information about a subject or an issue that has already been well-studied. At a higher level however, research can present new knowledge and can also use that knowledge to address uncertain, inconsistent or problematical phenomena. Finally, at an even higher level research can challenge or even upset widely held assumptions or accepted answers to a particular question.

Box 2.6. Stage 5 examples

1. *Changes in attitude towards the idea of 'kingship' in Nepal in the period 1920–1990 resulted in the erosion of political consensus within the country.*
2. *There is a connection that can be established between the lack of development of the railway system in Brazil (when compared to other South American countries) and the political agenda of the British government in the middle of the nineteenth century.*

Stage 6: Qualifying claims

Once you have decided that you have found a claim or thesis that is both specific and significant, you will need to consider its precise wording. In particular, you must determine whether it needs to be qualified in some way, either by adding certain limiting conditions to it or by hedging.

Box 2.7. Examples of conditional claims

1. *It will be argued that the 1989 'velvet revolution' in the former Czechoslovakia has brought considerable economic benefits to all sections of society, <u>provided that the cases of those with military pensions are excluded from this analysis</u>.*
This recognizes the fact that economic benefits have not been shared evenly across Czech society, with pensioners suffering the greatest disadvantages.
2. *We can conclude that the famine in North Korea in the late 1990s was more widespread than has been reported, <u>assuming that the testimony presented by refugees is considered to be reliable</u>.*
This acknowledges the fact that the main evidence for this conclusion has been provided by refugees and that other perspectives are not available, thus limiting the scope of the analysis.

For some writers it is a real liberation to realize that the claims which are being made need not be absolute but may be made subject to such conditions or provisions. Thus, 'I will claim that X is true only under the following conditions....'

The term 'hedging' refers to the skilful use of language to soften the force of an argument, making it clear that absolute certainty is not attached to a particular claim. For further explanation see, for example, Hyland (1995) or Holliday (2002: 179). This feature of academic writing will also be explored in more detail in Chapter 9.

Box 2.8. Examples of hedged claims

1. *<u>We suggest</u> that the recent social unrest in rural communities in France <u>may possibly be due</u> to problems which predate the recent arrival of wealthy Britons acquiring holiday homes.*
Uncertainty concerning the reasons for social unrest is reflected in the use of tentative language such as 'suggest' rather than 'argue'. The addition of 'possibly' makes the statement even more tentative.
2. *The rapid spread of Spanish in many urban communities in the southern United States <u>would appear to support the argument</u> that these parts of the country <u>can begin to be considered</u> truly bilingual.*
Here the modals 'would' and 'can' and the verb 'appear' all soften the force of the argument.

It should be noted that the effect of excessive hedging or too many conditions will be to weaken the strength of the claim to the point may seem unjustified. In addition, too many qualifiers can cause ambiguity or a lack of clarity. Consider the following:

Box 2.9. Examples of unsuccessful hedging

1. *Despite claims made by the government that Bulgaria is undergoing educational reform, what is really happening is a return to pre-World War 2 traditions – a step backwards rather than forwards.*
   This would almost certainly be regarded as too strong a claim to be sustained, with the last phrase *'a step backwards rather than forwards'* a seemingly unnecessary addition.
2. *It might be suggested that the Bulgarian government might possibly not be engaged in educational reform. Instead, it is conceivable that what may be happening is a possible return to pre-WW2 traditions.*
   This hedges the evidence using language that conveys the uncertainty of the underlying claim. But it goes too far, making the actual claim unclear and irritating the reader with the repetition of 'might' and 'possibly/possible'.

▶ Developing an updated rationale for the research

Role of the research rationale
A written rationale which builds on the original research proposal (see Chapter 1) has an important role to play in the initial stages of research for the following reasons:

- It can act as a very useful point of reference, aiding communication with supervisors, helping to keep discussions more focused and also to map progress up to a particular point.
- It can help with the exploration, clarification and definition of key concepts.
- It can act as a 'justifying document', representing the first attempts at establishing the significance of the research for a specified group of readers.
- A 'rolling rationale' can provide a record of a researcher's thinking at a particular stage of a project. At various points in the future, it will be

necessary to reconnect with previous thinking and the way in which ideas have developed over a period of time. In its final form, it can be summarized as the research project abstract.

A proposed structure

How should such a rationale be structured? There are many possible ways of approaching this. The following elements are likely to appear in some form:

- a brief presentation of the research context
- research aims and questions (as far as this is possible at this stage)
- a consideration of the significance of the research aims and questions
- a brief overview of the research methodology and data collection methods
- anticipated findings (as far as possible)

Rojon and Saunders (2012) have suggested a number of questions for evaluating such a rationale, including the following:

- whether the research project 'adds value' either by exploring a completely new topic or by providing fresh insights into an old topic
- whether the research project can demonstrate strong links to relevant theory and related literature
- whether the research aims and objectives meet the criteria of being 'transparent, specific, relevant, interconnected, answerable and measurable'

Task 2.4: An updated research rationale

A template for the updated rationale can be found in Appendix 3. These are some of the questions that you may wish to consider beforehand:

1. How can I provide clear boundaries for the context of my research?
2. How can I specify research aims if they are not entirely clear at this stage?
3. How can I formulate research questions? How many questions should I include?
4. How can I explain and justify the proposed design of the research and its procedures for data collection and analysis?
5. To what extent can my research be justified? What arguments can I put forward to identify its significance?

There are no 'right answers' to such questions. However, they will be of considerable assistance when you discuss the development of your research topic with your supervisors and peers.

Action Points

1. Consider the <u>feasibility</u> of your proposed research topic. Discuss with a supervisor whether it will be manageable in its current form within the time available.
2. Consider the <u>specificity</u> of your topic: break it down so that its focus becomes clearer. This breakdown can be effectively achieved by combining lateral and linear approaches.
3. Consider the <u>significance</u> of your topic: through a mix of reading, writing and discussion activities, ensure that your research contributes to your field of study.
4. <u>Develop research questions and claims</u> carefully and thoughtfully: your first intuitive efforts may need to be reconsidered.
5. Pay attention to the <u>wording of any claims or hypotheses</u>: even a slight change to the wording may fundamentally change your argument.
6. Throughout the whole process of research topic development, keep writing: gradually <u>build up a revised rationale</u> that will act as a point of reference for the entire research project.

3 Managing Research Reading

This chapter

- *examines the relationship between research reading and writing*
- *considers different reading aims within a research project*
- *identifies problem areas related to text selection*
- *compares different 'levels' of reading, contrasting reading to understand and/or to summarize content with reading in order to respond to ideas via critical analysis*
- *considers specific reading-to-writing tasks, including summarizing, paraphrasing and critical notetaking*

▶ Reading aims

The first piece of general advice that supervisors give to PhD researchers is very often to 'go away and read'. When such advice is given and received, it seems straightforward enough. But in practice, it can have very different meanings for different individuals. It can for some readers mean a green light that signals the starting point of a long and convoluted process of jumping from text to text, following a reference provided by one text leading to another – and then another. In this way it is possible for the reader to reach a point which is very far from where they first started without realizing precisely how this has happened. It can also mean unintentionally completing a circle or series of circles and returning to the point of departure. This type of process can be immensely frustrating: taken to extremes, it can also prove to be both ineffective and unproductive.

My own experience of reading for a PhD in the early 1990s seems typical. My approach to reading was very simple: I calculated that if I summarized everything that I identified as important, I would inevitably have valuable material that could be used in my writing. Following this logic it is possible to read 20 articles (or 30 or 40) and to file 20 or more summaries without too many problems or without really thinking. Then inevitably, a point is reached where decisions have to be made concerning what to do with all of the material that has been collected and carefully filed under each author's name. I can remember very clearly reaching this point and realizing that this type of approach was not taking me very far, but not really knowing how I could find an alternative that would be truly effective.

A further problem is that producing multiple summaries of other peoples' work does not just lead to a dead end; in the worst cases, it can be seriously counterproductive. The danger of the summary is that it takes the reader away from the original text and can easily involve the distortion or misrepresentation of ideas that are being presented. Such misinterpretations can occur either at the time when the summary is produced, or later when the summary is re-examined separately from the original text. One distortion of facts or ideas can lead to another. Invalid conclusions may be produced because they are based on a summary which is itself invalid.

Early stages of reading

What supervisors usually mean when they say 'go away and read' is for the reader to begin to read in a gentle exploratory mode, getting a feel for the topic of the research project even when this may have been defined in advance by a supervisory team. At this stage the aim is not to provide a complete overview of everything that is out there but rather to <u>follow leads related to the proposed topic</u>. The idea is that the more we read, the more we will clarify our thinking. But very often the reverse is true – the more we read, the more confused we can become. This experience is summed up by these researchers:

> Reading on topics related to the research or on the research topic itself contracts and expands the area of focus, making it difficult to pinpoint exactly what it is that you are studying. The object is amorphous and constantly changing.
>
> I'm having difficulties narrowing my focus and not making this a PhD about everything. Everything I research seems connected to so much else. It is hard to define boundaries and stick to them.
>
> The problem I have is self-made because I became interested in a sub-branch of my thesis and need to rein myself back.

To prevent exploratory reading from running out of control, it may be useful to bear in mind the image of entering an ongoing debate. What we are attempting can be seen as the equivalent of walking into a room filled with people engaged in animated conversations and gradually tuning in to one or more of the conversations that are taking place. We can, if we wish, flit from one conversation to another, though this is unlikely to make any of them particularly meaningful. Alternatively, we can spend a longer amount of time eavesdropping before deciding on the precise moment when we feel ready and confident enough to join in. In each case we are not just focusing on what is being said but also attempting to establish the parameters of the debate that is taking place.

This analogy can be taken only so far. It is clear that discussion and debate involving the written word are very different from a rapid interchange of ideas. Sometimes it is possible to identify a focused debate that takes place over a number of years with one writer responding to an article written by another, and possibly a third writer responding to both. In general, however, it takes time and effort to discover the different strands of a particular debate written by authors who sometimes may not even be aware of the existence of another text promoting very different views. It is the reader's task to try to join together the strands before considering all arguments on merit and then joining the debate through writing. This is one of the primary purposes of the literature review, discussed in the next chapter.

A second aim of exploratory reading is to help generate new research questions, which can then be tested for significance through further reading. Chapter 2 describes this process in detail. A third aim is to begin to unpack key concepts relevant to the research. These tend to fall into two categories – more technical concepts and those that appear on first examination to be nontechnical in nature. Chapter 5 deals with the exploration of such concepts through reading and writing.

Finally, exploratory reading also has the advantage that it helps build what Rugg and Petre (2004: 55) refer to as 'the researcher's core literature'. These authors argue that most researchers carry round in their memory 'a good accessible database of relevant papers' that can be valuable for many years. A 'core literature' is also accompanied by a core bibliography which can act as an important reference source for the duration of a PhD research project and beyond.

Later stages of reading

At a certain point, exploratory reading needs to end. Once the research topic has been developed by following the kinds of procedures described in Chapter 2, it is both possible and necessary to approach reading in a much more focused way. This is the time for you to start trying out specific questions to see where they lead when compared to the work of other researchers, to begin to test your claims or hypotheses, to investigate whether others have asked similar questions or posited similar claims and, if so, what types of answers or results were obtained. Another approach might consist of investigating whether your proposed research questions have already been considered in a different context. Similarly, it is worth finding out whether the claims or hypotheses that you are putting forward have been tested by other writers and, if so, with what results. The quality and quantity of evidence supporting claims made by writers also need to be carefully researched. Finally, it is clearly important to look for counterclaims and counterevidence so that all sides of a particular debate can be represented.

This process does not, however, imply a suppression of your own voice. An important consequence of this type of exercise is that you will be able to position yourself somewhere within the debate with growing levels of authority, strengthening your stance as you conduct a careful analysis of your reading. Booth, Colomb & Williams (1995: 95) describe this type of reading in these terms:

> *When you read, be generous. Read first to understand fully. Go slowly: re-read passages that puzzle or confuse you. If you cannot summarize a passage in your mind, assume you don't understand it well enough to use it as an argument. Don't start by assuming that you have to disagree with everything you find. In this first reading, resolve ambiguities in favour of the source. But once you understand a source, you are free to disagree.*

Deciding when exploratory reading needs to end and more focused reading needs to begin requires very careful consideration. There is always a danger of narrowing the focus of research reading too soon, just as there is with the choice of research questions (see Chapter 2). To ensure that the focus is right, some readers prefer to go back to exploratory mode from time to time – an approach which is especially useful if completely new ideas emerge from reading or from discussions with supervisors or peers.

▶ Problem areas associated with reading

This section considers some of the main problem areas involved in the management of your reading, together with some effective strategies for dealing with them. For an examination of the problems that readers may experience in understanding the style of certain academic texts, see Chapter 9.

Access to sources

In the pre-digital age the problem was often one of lack of availability of source materials, especially if speedy access was required. Inter-library loans were an important means of obtaining texts not available locally, but these could sometimes take weeks or even months. Journals provided indexes that necessitated time-consuming manual searches.

Now it seems that the problem is the direct opposite. On one website alone (the British Library's Electronic Theses Online Service – EThOS), it is possible to search through almost all of the PhD theses completed in the UK in recent years and to download many of them free of charge. At the time of writing there were 400,000 entries with over 150,000 offering access to the full thesis text. The British Library, as part of the EThOS project, has also digitized a large number of older theses so that the range could be expanded even more. For details, see http://www.ethos.ac.uk/.

How do you cope with this power at your fingertips? With such abundance, clear selection criteria will need to be applied on a consistent basis.

Establishing selection criteria

At the start of a PhD research project, it may be the case that you have no clearly defined criteria for deciding which texts require close attention and which texts can be rejected. As a result, you may find yourself inadvertently doing some or all of the following:

- reading very slowly and producing few meaningful notes
- reading each text in exactly the same way and at the same speed
- reading everything twice or three times to make sure it is understood
- giving equal attention to each sentence and each paragraph within a text
- taking notes in an identical way for each text
- summarizing texts in a similar way after careful reading

However, even a momentary pause for thought is enough to realize that these types of procedures may not be productive. Certain texts (those identified as key texts) are bound to be more significant than others. It is also likely that other texts will produce only one or two useful items – a quotation, a single argument, a set of statistics or even a diagram or table. Furthermore, there are texts that might be considered 'possible texts' when we realize that our attitude towards them might change at some point. This is true even for those texts that appear to be 'impossible', with no obvious relevance or quality. The different levels might be summarized as follows:

Box 3.1. Categorization of reading texts

'Seminal'
A text of such importance that it is required reading in a particular area

'Key' (or 'Important')
A text that merits detailed reading and understanding

'Useful'
A text that contains more than one interesting or useful idea

'Single item'
A text that contains one useful fact, argument, quotation or illustrative example

'Possible'
A text that might be useful in the future

'Impossible'
A text that can be rejected at this stage

At the top of my categorization is the **seminal text**. This is the one that you believe you have to read because it contains original thinking relevant to the research topic and has influenced many other writers. You may not need to read it in its entirety, but you have at least to acknowledge its existence. A text might be considered seminal not just in terms of its specific content: it could, for instance, have been written by the person who first proposed the theoretical framework that underpins much of your analysis. To sum up, it may not be your most valuable text, but it is considered a significant point of reference. Some examples in specific fields might include Edward Said's *Orientalism* in anthropology or history (1978), or Noam Chomsky's *Aspects of the Theory of Syntax* in linguistics (1965).

A **key (important) text** is one that you read intensively, paying attention to more or less every word and every paragraph. Almost every section of this type of text may be considered to be of value. Intensive reading implies that you have already decided that this text is going to be important for your research, and you propose to examine all the different elements with the aim of extracting valuable and relevant arguments, interesting quotations, facts or summative analysis. Sometimes it is hard to identify really important texts of this type. One certainty is that over a period of time your thinking will change with respect to their importance or lack of importance. For instance, it is possible to look at a text in the early stages of research and think that it can play a key role in your analysis, only to discover later that it is based on another text which is of greater significance. It may also be the case that a later reading begins to give the impression that the arguments are rather shallow or the evidence is thin. Conversely, you can look at a text and wonder whether it is of interest or not. One useful test might be to highlight interesting ideas or facts and then consider their number and their significance. The more that you are highlighting, the more likely it is to be important.

The **useful text** is one that does not need to be read intensively from beginning to end but contains a number of valuable elements in certain sections, such as a series of arguments, powerful quotations, tables, diagrams or sets of statistics. In my invented selection system, I find that many texts tend to fall into this category, at least initially. Often, however, they will be downgraded or upgraded to 'key' status at a later date.

The **single item text** is self-explanatory. Its identified purpose is to provide you with just one usable argument, counterargument, fact, quotation, picture or diagram. In my experience, many texts tend to be located in this category. This is where very careful records are required: it is easy to forget a reference when the rest of the text may appear to be completely irrelevant. It is also worth noting that the single item might just be a further reference in the bibliography attached to the text itself.

A **possible text** is one that you are not sure about but are unwilling to reject, as you believe that it might be helpful in some way. Such texts may or may not be upgraded at a later date.

Finally, there are **impossible texts**, which do not appear to have anything to offer. Before the text is discarded, bear in mind that your thinking might change. The text may be discarded, but the fact that you have considered it must not be forgotten. Record the reference carefully and store it for future reference.

Leaving your footprints

Every time you read a text, you will need to leave tracks to show that you have been there – tracks that you will recognize if you return to the same text at a later date. For PhD research, I believe that this of particular importance as the gap between a first reading and a later reading of the same text might be a month, a year or even much longer.

A familiar past experience for me has been returning to a text and immediately asking myself questions such as, 'Have I been here before? When exactly? Did I mark my presence in any way? What did I think about this text? What decisions did I take as a result of reading it?' If it is possible to return to a text and find clear answers to such questions, this can provide a direct communication channel to a previous way of thinking.

Footprints can be left in a number of ways. At a very simple level, we can highlight facts or ideas with a coloured marker or a collection of coloured pens. We can summarize and then synthesize important ideas. We can query text content, compare one text to another, write and file analytical notes which make our reaction to the text very clear. All of this can help us demonstrate to ourselves that a text is valuable in some way or that it lacks value. This is the evidence that we can refer back to that shows that we have read something and understood its importance and its relevance to our research.

To revisit a text after a period of time, we need to understand and reconsider our first impressions. We may discover that they have not changed or that they need to be updated. There are even significant occasions when we realize that our very first impressions now seem to be 'the right ones', with later changes in thinking suddenly seeming misguided. Whatever the changes in our thinking may be as we read, we need to keep track of all of them, particularly with reference to key texts.

To sum up, every time we read a text we are doing so at a particular stage in the development of our own thinking. It can be confidently predicted that reading the same text in six months' time will be a different experience. Recording the *narrative of our thinking* is a crucial aspect of any research project, but is of particular importance in PhD work which can take many years to complete.

Applying the selection criteria

How is it possible for you to decide whether a text is really important for your research? And how can you overcome the understandable fear of missing something vital? There are a number of possible indicators. For instance, research papers can provide many clues to the content of a text and quality of analysis by means of the abstract. In other texts, indicators can include the introductory and concluding sections and even the topic sentences that begin paragraphs in structured writing. A paper can be skimmed by just focusing on these clues, and thus an initial assessment can be made: if the decision is to read the text more carefully, this decision can always be reversed. However, if every sentence of every paragraph is assumed to have equal merit, this will clearly lead to an approach to reading which is both ineffective and probably unproductive as well. The majority of texts listed in a bibliography may well turn out to be 'single item', with the rest of the text discarded.

The following introductory paragraph of a briefing paper produced by a team of academics is presented in a way that is likely to help the reader make an informed decision concerning its importance and relevance. Each paragraph is introduced by a topic sentence (which I have underlined). Each topic sentence acts as a clear indicator of the arguments that will be developed within the paragraph. Each paragraph adds new information by means of the topic sentence. Finally, the topic sentences can be read in sequence indicating the direction in which the argumentation is being developed:

Box 3.2. Exploring the Links between Climate Change, Agriculture and Development: A briefing paper

Key messages

<u>The scale of the challenges posed by climate change requires urgent action</u>. Agriculture is both a major cause of global warming, and will be significantly affected by it. More demands are now being placed upon agriculture: global food security, responding to climate change, protecting environmental services. This presents both challenges and opportunities to policy-makers and practitioners.

<u>Many climate change adaptation or mitigation initiatives have been project-based activities – but this is insufficient</u>. Climate change responses require more coordinated action amongst relevant stakeholders across different scales. Planning and capacity strengthening has to be integrated into government policy-making in a coherent fashion. Responding to climate change requires consideration of the implications for trade flows as well as production impacts. Economic models may need to be revisited. Climate change challenges need to be understood as they interact with other major development processes (e.g. globalisation, de-agrarianisation, urbanisation, migration).

<u>More integrated or holistic conceptual frameworks have emerged in recent years</u>, which seek to combine more specific climate change responses (e.g. particular mitigation technologies) with shorter and longer term *development* objectives. Proponents of existing concepts, such as sustainable agriculture, increasingly recognize climate change issues. The green economy concept suggests that future economic development and the securing of environmental services are intertwined. In the agricultural sector, the broad concept of Climate Smart Agriculture is moving to the fore. It merges productivity, adaptation, mitigation and climate resilience, alongside broader development goals.

<u>There is a crowded field of climate change and related concepts which jostle for attention</u>. Each concept has its own promoters and opponents – some more powerful than others. The broad nature of the concepts

→

allows for varied interpretations in implementation, encourages inclusiveness and sparks debate. Conversely broad definitions risk masking real differences in development visions including questions of participation, power and equity, the forms of technology and institutions involved, the role of markets and national autonomy. Too open a definition could prevent recognition of the need for more game changing action.

Making these concepts operational presents many challenges, not the least of which are building consensus, creating the right incentives and enabling conditions. Climate change may only be adding to the challenges facing agriculture, but it could also act as a catalyst, alongside other global concerns, to create fresh opportunities for sustainable agricultural development.

Nelson, V. & Lamboll, R. 2012, Briefing Paper: Climate Learning for African Agriculture, Natural Resources Unit, University of Greenwich

Critical and 'non-critical' reading

A major problem area recognized by PhD writers is the need to establish a strong connection between research reading and research writing. At the beginning of this chapter, I described my own experiences in this respect and endorsed the need for an approach that will take the reader beyond merely recording and summarizing what is being said by each author. To develop such an approach, a useful starting point might be to consider two distinct levels or modes of reading, as specified below. In the rest of this chapter, I will refer to these as 'Level 1' and 'Level 2' reading. Their basic characteristics are as follows.

Level 1: 'Surface reading'

Reading at a more superficial level involves achieving a basic understanding of all or part of the content of a text. Typical tasks can include:

- picking out main arguments or identifying a writer's stance
- identifying specific information such as evidence underpinning an argument
- brief summaries of important sections of text

In addition, Level 1 reading can also involve a mix of strategies such as:

- predicting the content of academic texts
- skimming for gist understanding

- scanning for specific ideas
- decoding complexity
- paraphrasing ideas
- referencing ideas
- synthesizing ideas

Level 2: Critical reading

At a higher level, reading involves not just understanding but also responding to ideas within a text via critical analysis. At the simplest level, this means questioning the ideas that are being presented. A question mark added to a piece of text can sometimes be more revealing than a summarized version of what the writer has to say, as it can signal very clearly to the returning reader that a sentence or paragraph requires more careful examination.

It is useful, however, to break down this type of questioning process into three distinct areas. The first concerns *examining a writer's stance* and in particular the following:

- identifying writer agendas that are explicit (overt)
- identifying writer agendas that are implicit (covert)
- locating a writer's perspective within one or more established paradigms

Sometimes, it can be useful to try to locate a writer's position within a particular school of thought or paradigm. Thody (2006: 100) supplies categories for this process by using broad labels such as 'political', 'religious', 'social', or 'postcolonialist', 'feminist' and 'postmodernist'. PhD researchers may feel that they are to some extent obliged to align authors to a particular school of thought in this way. It should be borne in mind, however, that this kind of labelling cannot be summative and that a justification of some sort for this kind of placement will be required.

The second approach towards critical reading is more complex in that it entails *an examination of different aspects of the logic and coherence of a writer's arguments.* There are many distinct possibilities here, such as:

- considering the validity of claims put forward by a writer
- identifying and commenting on any 'hidden' assumptions underlying claims
- considering arguments arising from the main claims
- examining different circumstances or contexts in which claims might be demonstrably true or false
- considering any generalizations based on claims

- considering the quantity and the quality of supporting evidence
- considering the validity of a writer's conclusions

This type of analysis can often be very productive when applied to a text that seems important and relevant to your research. It is very unusual for an entire text to be deeply flawed, but it is more common for there to be a single but significant flaw in the arguments. The starting point is to consider any claims that are being put forward and to examine carefully whether any questionable assumptions are built in. A very simple example of this can be seen below:

**Box 3.3. Examining assumptions
that underlie a claim**

'Tourism is beneficial to developing nations in a number of ways'

First assumption: readers will have a shared understanding of what 'tourism' includes and excludes.
Second assumption: readers will have a shared understanding of the meaning of 'developing' and will be in agreement concerning which nations can be classified as such.
Third assumption: 'a number of ways' might include social and cultural as well as economic benefits.

Sometimes impressive-sounding language may hide a flimsy claim or argument or a lack of substantial supporting evidence. When assessing complex texts in terms of their importance and relevance for our research, we will need to realize that a particular text can only make a significant contribution to the debate either when we can show that the arguments are robust or when it is our deliberate intention to demonstrate that the arguments are flawed. The validity of arguments and the conclusions drawn from them are, of course, subject to debate, and in the latter case, we will need to demonstrate a discontinuity or contradiction of some sort, asking ourselves questions such as, 'How do arguments presented within a text compare with the initial premise or claim made earlier?'

Booth, Colomb and Williams (1995: 72–3) have produced a useful overview for disagreeing with the claims made by source materials. This includes a specification of different types of contradictions that can be detected. For example, you can argue that:

- X cannot always be placed in category Y
- X cannot necessarily be considered part of Y
- X cannot be considered as a further development of Y
- X does not cause Y
- Though X appears to cause Y, it also has other significant consequences
- Though X may be true in one context, this may not be the case elsewhere

The third approach within Level 2 reading involves *an examination of the use of language* by authors and a consideration of its effects (whether intended or unintended). Questions that we might usefully ask ourselves here include the following:

- Is the author exaggerating? In what respects?
- Is the author making use of vague language? For what purpose(s)?
- Are there any ambiguities in the language used? Do these appear to be intentional or unintentional?
- Does the use of language affect the quality of the claims being made? Do claims need to be modified or hedged as a result?

Critical reading skills across cultures

In my experience, a question that often arises is whether critical reading skills are easy to develop if the reader has been educated within a different tradition. The comment of one researcher is typical in this respect when she states that 'It is very hard for me to read something and then question it because I was raised in a way to not question. When it says "academic article", I fear saying that this is wrong.'

One problem is that when we read a text that seems difficult, our automatic reaction is, if I cannot understand the argument, then it must somehow be my fault. We will need to examine this assumption more carefully because difficulty could equally be the consequence of ambiguity or even obfuscation in the writing itself. See Chapter 9 for a more detailed discussion of what could be considered 'difficult language' within academic texts.

At the same time, the thinking that underpins critical reading needs to be examined, as there are variations in the understanding of 'critical thinking' in different cultures. In particular, the negative connotations of 'critical' and 'criticism' need to be considered. Critical thinking appears to exist everywhere in some form, across cultures and across disciplinary areas. However, the *norms of critical analysis* may be different. When conducting research in a different culture, it is essential to be fully aware of these norms and expectations, both when reading and also when writing for your own readers. A clear breakdown of the concept as it is understood across many higher education environments is provided by Cottrell (2005: 2).

▶ Notetaking: From reading into writing

In this section, we examine ways in which the development of reading strategies can provide a series of direct links between reading and writing. A range of different ways of recording reading will also be presented for consideration.

Level 1 notetaking

Earlier, it was argued that Level 1 reading involves achieving a basic understanding of all or part of the content of a text. As a result, typical notetaking tasks at this level might include any of the following:

- writing a short summary of the main arguments or facts presented
- selecting more detailed information in response to specific questions
- extracting a quotation to illustrate a particular point
- paraphrasing of ideas presented within the text
- synthesizing of ideas presented in different parts of the text

---

Box 3.4. Typical Level 1 questions

1. What claims are being made in this text? Where are the claims stated?
2. What evidence has been produced to support the claims?
3. What conclusions have been drawn based on the evidence?

Notetaking at Level 1 can serve multiple purposes. Wallace (2004: 165) provides a useful overview of these, ranging from situations in which the reader needs to remember something very precisely to those where the aim is to be much more selective in what is recorded. At one extreme, we can note down exact words in the form of a quotation; at the other we summarize or paraphrase one particular piece of information. In between the two, we may find ourselves taking a greater interest in some parts of the text than others. The same author also claims that interacting with a text in such ways is likely to make it more memorable. If a text becomes memorable, there is a greater likelihood that we can put it to productive use at a later stage.

Notetaking at this level can involve the reprocessing of information in a number of different ways, the most conspicuous of these being *summarizing*, *paraphrasing* and *synthesizing*.

Summarizing

According to Swales and Feak (1994: 105), a good summary should:

1. offer a *balanced* coverage of the original
2. present the source material in a *neutral* fashion
3. *condense* the source material and be presented in the summary writer's *own words*

This is sound advice. At this level, as I have noted previously, it is important that there is no distortion (whether deliberate or inadvertent) of a writer's views. The selection or exclusion of information must produce a text shorter than the original but one which preserves the balance of the original argumentation. If counterarguments, for instance, are carefully considered in the original, this would normally need to be reflected in the summarized version. If a range of evidence from different sources is mentioned in the original, this also needs to be acknowledged in the summarized version. As far as possible, the summarized text will need to be presented with a clear emphasis on views expressed by the original writer, with the views of the summarizer being excluded.

Achieving a 'neutral' tone within a summary is, however, not as easy as it sounds. Variations in language used by summarizers can alter the writer's original views in subtle ways. There is no perfect solution to this: the summarizer's use of his or her own words will inevitably alter the tone of the original text to some extent. What is important is to keep this in mind and to check and, if necessary, re-edit text summaries very carefully.

A final point to bear in mind is that there are occasions in which a summarizer may actually improve the clarity of the original text, such as in cases where there is significant repetition, excessive use of imagery or exemplification, gratuitous use of jargon, redundancy or obscurity.

Paraphrasing

The act of paraphrasing involves the restating of another writer's ideas in your own words. The ideas remain theirs and will need to be acknowledged, while the choice of the precise wording is yours. Paraphrasing is in itself not a particularly problematic process. The difficulty lies in choosing when to paraphrase rather than quote a writer's words directly.

Booth, Colomb and Williams (1995: 207) recommend the use of paraphrase when you are more interested in the actual nature of findings rather than in how a source expresses them. For these authors, direct quotations are more relevant when either the authority of the source writer or the exact words are seen to be significant. Two additional reasons for preferring paraphrased versions of events are suggested:

- In many cases, you will be able to express more clearly than the original author the key ideas that you wish to convey to your intended readers.
- You will also wish to avoid any accusation of writing in a derivative and unoriginal fashion. Frequent verbatim quotations from other writers could easily be regarded in this way.

Synthesizing

Synthesizing in relation to research writing involves the combining of ideas or information either from within a single source text or across a range of texts. Here is an example:

Box 3.5. Synthesizing different source references

Source 1: Billig (2013) claims that the use of a large amount of technical terminology may be convenient for certain academic writers, but very often 'ordinary words' can be used to greater effect since ideas can be communicated more quickly and more effectively.

Source 2: According to Culler (2003), intellectual effort is required on the part of the readers of 'difficult' academic texts. The writer cannot be reasonably expected to make every argument 100 per cent clear for every reader.

Source 3: Butler (2003) argues that language has an important role in taking the reader away from common 'frames of reference', enabling us to see the world in new ways.

<u>Possible synthesis</u>: 'While authors such as Billig (2013) criticize stylistic excess in academic writing, others (for example Culler 2003, Butler 2003) argue that "difficult writing" cannot always be considered an unreasonable burden on readers and is often fully justifiable'.

It might be argued that producing a synthesis of this type goes beyond our previous definition of Level 1 reading. Summarizing different texts and then combining or comparing them does appear to provide a bridge between Level 1 and Level 2 reading activities as the synthesizing process can often lead directly into critical analysis.

Level 2 notetaking

At Level 2, notetaking begins to involve different kinds of critical analysis, such as:

- highlighting and then interpreting key points or quotes
- identifying specific arguments and key issues which have a particular relevance to the research project
- annotating the text with your own critical comments on specific points
- drawing conclusions from these comments and presenting them in a summarized form
- obtaining analysis which is directly linked to arguments within the text itself and therefore not based on a summarized version removed from the original
- commenting on language used to express arguments, especially emotive language, rhetoric, exaggeration and vague or non-specific terms

---

Box 3.6. Typical Level 2 questions

1. What are your views on the value of the claims being made? Do you agree or partially agree with them? On what grounds?
2. What are your views on the value of the evidence presented?
3. What are your views on any conclusions that are being drawn?
4. How do the arguments presented compare with those of other authors?
5. How do the arguments presented compare with your own thinking?
6. Overall, how impressed are you with the quality of the arguments presented? Do you find them convincing or not?

A typical Level 2 notetaking sequence

Notetaking usually begins with the highlighting of key points or quotations. For Level 2 reading, the second and most important step is to begin to formulate a response to these. The kind of questions we might ask ourselves at this stage can be expected to result in notes that begin to form the basis of critical analysis as follows:

1. This is what this author has to say on the particular issue that interests me.
2. These seem to be the underlying reason(s).
3. This is the evidence supporting the reasons.
4. This could be said to be the author's stance.
5. This is my reaction to the basic claim or premise.
6. This is my reaction to the development of the arguments (logical? flawed?).
7. This is my reaction to the evidence presented.
8. This is my reaction to the conclusions drawn.

Even if the comment is in the form of a question mark, or simply records that something looks interesting or that you agree or disagree with what is being said, this can give some indication of your thinking at a particular point in time.

The following extract from a research proposal at Master's level shows how this approach might work in practice. The first step is to highlight or shade the key points that are being made. The second is to add analytic comments in response to these arguments:

Box 3.7. Annotating a reading text with analytical comments

In the last decade, the influx of Chinese students in UK institutions of higher education has increased immensely. These students, upon arrival in the UK, face a culture different from their own and they need to deal with problems of adjustment, both from a sociocultural as well as an educational point of view.

The impact of all the unfamiliar experiences that Chinese students face is connected with the terms of Culture Shock and Learning Shock. The shock occurs in terms of changing places and cultural transition since China and the UK are two very different countries. During this transition, Chinese students encounter pedagogical, sociocultural and

Are Culture Shock and Learning Shock completely separate phenomena? Or can one be included in the other?

→

psychological challenges, all of which are equally important. Nonetheless, in this dissertation I will focus only on the pedagogical challenges and the Chinese students' adjustment with regard to the British academic culture.

> Important to them? To others?

Based on Clark's identification of three broad value systems permeating the contemporary educational process (1987), Classical Humanism, Reconstructionism and Progressivism, I will refer to the Educational Value Systems of the two countries and highlight the differences that cause difficulties in the Chinese students' academic adjustment. I will further analyse specific cultural values that are inextricably linked with the Chinese students as individuals and their importance in shaping these students' attitudes and learning practices. Some of the difficulties faced when trying to culturally adjust to teaching and learning in a British University include critical thinking, learner autonomy, plagiarism, classroom participation, and assessment. I will particularly focus on autonomy, participation and assessment while linking them with the educational and cultural values.

> Are these equally problematic for all Chinese students? And is the order random or in order of difficulty?

Chinese students' thinking, classroom behaviour and learning styles have been influenced and shaped by cultural values and beliefs that are not the same as those of Western countries. More precisely, Western 'cultures' of teaching and approaches to learning tend to focus and give priority and importance to student-centeredness, critical thinking and application of knowledge, whereas the Chinese ones tend to emphasize teacher-centeredness, rote learning and memorization. Consequently, the Chinese students who arrive for studies in the UK encounter difficulties, since approaches and methods to teaching and learning differ significantly.

> Is it problematic to group all 'Western' countries together?

The Chinese educational system has been highly influenced by the Confucian cultural heritage, which is a critical element of the Chinese cultural identity. Confucianism operates within a hierarchically orientated

> Is this cultural identity stable or in the process of being changed?

> society some characteristics of which are respect of authority, emphasis on the family and traditional educational methods, preservation of harmony and avoidance of losing face. All of these have implications when it comes to teaching and learning in a British educational context and they will all be analysed in detail in the following chapter. In order to facilitate a better understanding of the cultural and educational differences between China and the UK, I will examine them within the analytical framework that Hofstede (1983) provides for comparing cultural values.

If you can annotate a key text with analytical comments of this type, the next stage could be to produce a summary at the end. This will be a summary of a different kind – not a condensed version of what the author of the text is saying but a summary of your considered response. The question that this kind of summary addresses will be simply, 'Am I convinced?'

An analytic summary can also take the reader beyond the text that is being examined. The resulting analysis might include a consideration of:

- how this author's stance appears to compare with those of others
- how your own views compare with those of other critics

For the extract above, you could add a short summary such as this one to your notes:

> It is difficult to avoid making generalizations with this kind of topic. The assumption concerning shared Western values seems particularly problematic (see Watkins and Biggs 1996), but the idea of shared Chinese values may be equally so. The Hofstede framework should provide a useful point of reference for comparing findings from this project with those of other studies.

What is being proposed here is very different from Level 1 reading. It involves a recognition that an important element of reading is writing to yourself, recording ideas as they occur to you. Ethnographers such as Hammersley and Atkinson (1983: 191–2) have long recognized this at the data collection stage when analytical notes are produced to be built into a written narrative. In this case, the kind of analytical summaries that are described above are sometimes referred to as 'in-process memos' (Emerson, Fretz and Shaw 1995: 103–5).

If a reader can produce analysis of this type while reading, the result might be a small but focused piece of writing that could even be directly transferable into a paragraph in a draft chapter. It is arguable that a Level 1 summary of what a writer has said could also be transposed, but its use and effectiveness in developing your own arguments would probably be considerably less. Once reading and critical analysis become simultaneous processes, it becomes a little easier to bridge the gap between reading and writing. We read in order to write: our task is to integrate what we read into the context of our own writing. We think to ourselves, 'At this particular point in time, this is my question, this is my reaction, this is my response'.

Action Points

1. Make sure that the early stages of reading are productive by defining the scope of your project as you develop your research topic. Do not allow exploratory reading to run out of control: develop your own selection criteria for categorizing texts in order of perceived importance.
2. Read to try out your research questions and test your hypotheses, and read for evidence to support and strengthen your arguments.
3. Read to summarize, paraphrase and synthesize (Level 1 reading). Read in order to formulate analysis in response to key texts (Level 2 reading).
4. Make use of abstracts, headings and topic sentences to access the content of texts.
5. Produce analytical notes and summaries to enable you to reconnect to texts: leave your footprints when reading key texts.
6. Make a note of everything that you read even in the case of texts that may seem inappropriate: your thinking might change in the future.

4 Producing a Literature Review

This chapter

- *examines the multiple purposes of a literature review within a PhD research project*
- *explores alternative approaches to compiling a literature review and identifies potential problem areas*
- *considers the following questions: What type of literature review do you need? What steps will you follow to manage and assemble the relevant literature? How will you record your reading? How will you integrate your notes into draft and final chapters?*

▶ The literature review as a process and a product

The term 'literature review' can mean different things to different people. Confusingly, it is commonly used to describe both a process and a product. As a process, it can involve any or all of the following while engaging with 'the literature':

- exploring and guiding the development of research topics
- testing research questions, claims and hypotheses
- examining counterclaims and alternative hypotheses
- identifying, exploring and defining key concepts
- exploring research methodologies
- examining other relevant research projects and case studies

Meanwhile in its capacity as the end product of such work, a literature review can be embedded within a thesis in a number of ways. Here are some of the more common alternatives:

- an introductory chapter, providing a broad context for your research with reference to relevant literature
- a designated chapter within your thesis (as is often the case at Master's level)
- a number of designated chapters or designated sections within different chapters
- a series of separate chapters each relating to different studies that are included in the PhD thesis

Whether you are using the term in its 'process' or in its 'product' sense, it is essential for you to *clarify the expectations of all the potential readers*, including supervisors, examiners or other academics within your particular field or associated fields. Such expectations can vary greatly and, if ignored, can lead to potential misunderstandings. If, for example, you are conducting cross-disciplinary research, you might experience different reactions from different readers. If you are following the 'papers model' of the PhD, producing a new study for each year of your research project, there may be an expectation that you will produce entirely separate literature reviews for each study or a requirement for them to be closely linked. Hence the need to negotiate what the literature review as product will look like and how the literature review as process will need to be undertaken.

▶ The purposes of a literature review

There are many potential sources of guidance available for producing successful literature reviews. Generic examples include the work of Hart (1998) and Ridley (2008). There are also useful discipline-specific guides, one example of which is considered below. One worrying aspect is that these sources of support contain a wide range of different interpretations of the purpose of a literature review and its significance within a research project. The apparent lack of agreement between writers might perhaps be expected when comparing discipline-specific books, but less so in sourcebooks aimed at the general reader. The result is a rather confusing picture for aspiring PhD writers.

To illustrate such differences and examine their implications, I conducted an exercise with a group of about 100 PhD research students in their first year of study spread over a period of one year. All were committed to producing a literature review as part of the early stages of PhD research in preparation for a significant milestone – their first supervisory board. Nearly all were uncertain how to approach the literature review as a process and the nature of their final product. Three sources of guidance were chosen, two of which can be considered generic while the other is discipline specific: Cresswell (2003) 'Research Design', *Sage Publications,* Dornyei (2007) 'Research Methods in

Applied Linguistics', *Oxford University Press* and Thody (2006) 'Writing and Presenting Research', *Sage Publications*. The groups of PhD students were asked to compare different interpretations by the three authors on the role of a literature review in a research project. They were also invited to respond to the definitions and indicate which ones they found to be most applicable to their own research. The most useful points resulting from this exercise are summarized just below.

Joining an ongoing debate or dialogue (Cresswell 2003: 30)

This was considered to be an essential component of any literature review. Your review provides you with an access point to a debate that is already going on around you. There is a clear implication that your voice will feature prominently in the review that you produce.

Revealing current understanding of your topic (Thody 2006: 92)

A literature review needs to provide an in-depth analysis of the work of other writers who have already conducted research in your topic area. Thody suggests that to some extent it should also 'pay homage to those who have gone before you'. However, participants felt that using this type of expression could easily be misinterpreted. There is a clear difference between acknowledging the contributions made by others while critically appraising them and offering unmitigated praise.

Providing a framework for establishing the significance of a study (Cresswell 2003: 30)

Another important function of any literature review is to establish the significance of your research project by placing it within a wider context. This cannot be achieved by simply demonstrating the range of your knowledge or ensuring that the review 'acts as a map of the terrain' (Dornyei 2007: 281). The primary aim of a review should be to survey source materials that are directly related to the research topic rather than a body of literature in a particular field. At the same time, participants felt that it is important to explain why some well-known authors in the field and familiar theories have not been included in a literature review. This helps to define the parameters of a more focused debate, whatever the field of study.

Justifying your research by showing that others have not researched your topic or researched it in the same way (Thody 2006: 91)

This is closely related to the question of establishing the significance of your research. A literature review provides you with a good opportunity to highlight research which has *not* taken place, as well as projects which have been completed. A carefully constructed review can enable you to identify important gaps in previous research that you intend to fill as a result of your own work.

The kind of exercise described above can act as a useful starting point in clarifying the expectations of your readers with respect to the literature-review process. You will need to consider carefully the different roles and purposes in the case of your own research. Identifying and clarifying your precise aims (and rejecting others) will also help in the management of your research reading and the transformation of your reading into first draft chapter writing.

▶ Alternative approaches to the literature review as product

In terms of the literature review as product (rather than process), there are also important decisions to be made. At an early stage of your research, you will need to consider four important questions:

* What kind of literature review will you need?
* Will you need to produce an interim as well as a final literature review?
* How can you ensure that your own voice is present in your literature review?
* How will you structure your literature review?

What kind of literature review will you need?
As noted at the beginning of this chapter, the literature review can take many different forms within the overall structure of your thesis. If, for instance, you are following the 'papers/publication' model of PhD research, each of the articles built into your thesis may require a separate literature review, as is the case for the researcher below. Note that, interestingly, one of the papers in this particular example can be co-authored:

Box 4.1. One Researcher's Experience

I need to do three literature reviews of about 3,000 words each within my three papers of 12,000 words. You need to be very clear. At the same time, you need to read for three different things – it's a lot of work. One literature review would be much easier. In this case, I need the same structure, but each literature review is short. For the co-authored paper we both decided to do the literature review, but it will be 70 per cent my responsibility.

At this point, it would be useful and informative to be able to present a comparison of types of literature review across disciplinary areas. However, there appear to be no definitive rules in this respect. The results of an online poll among a group of 16 PhD researchers in their first year of study reveal the following:

Table 4.1 Literature reviews across disciplines

Disciplinary Area	Type of Literature Review	Separate Methodology Review?
Computer science	a) A designated chapter beginning with historical background	No
	b) Spread over several chapters	Yes
History	a) An interim literature review, uncertain about the final version	Yes
	b) Part of the introductory chapter and then throughout the text	Yes
Linguistics	a) Spread over several chapters	Undecided
	b) Part of an introductory chapter	No
	c) One designated chapter structured by themes	Yes
	d) Spread over several chapters	Yes
Literature	a) An interim literature review, uncertain about the final version	No
	b) Part of the introductory chapter	No
Management	a) A designated chapter	Yes
	b) A designated chapter	Yes
Psychology	a) A designated chapter structured by themes	Yes
	b) A designated chapter	No
	c) Separate literature reviews for different research papers included in my thesis	Yes
Sociology	a) An interim literature review, uncertain about the final version	No

Even with such small numbers, there appears to be great variance within all disciplines except for management researchers. In areas where variance exists, it is not difficult to find an explanation. For example, 'linguistics' could include researchers describing structural aspects of language (grammarians), social aspects of language (sociolinguistics) or language learning and teaching (psycholinguists, applied linguists). It is also clear that some respondents are still uncertain about some aspects of their literature review.

The decision to include or exclude a separate 'methodology literature review' is an important one. In some disciplines, it is likely that research methods and procedures will be of as much interest as the findings themselves. Readers may carefully study the design of experiments in order to adopt or adapt them for their own use. In some cases, the aim could even be replication, the task of the reader being to identify suitable procedures so that they can be tried out and their merits and demerits fully discussed.

The conclusions to be drawn are as follows:

a) Disciplinary norms and conventions will need to be referred to before you decide on your approach.
b) There is, however, no guarantee that there will be one well-established route to success within your disciplinary area. Instead, there may be different types of conventions for different types of projects.
c) In some cases, you may be free to plan the kind of literature review that you feel will match your research project aims; in others, a prescribed structure and approach may be laid down.
d) The question, 'what type of literature review do I need?' may therefore have no simple and straightforward answer.

The interim literature review

In the early stages of PhD work, it is likely that you will be asked to provide some evidence that your research is making progress. An interim literature review is a good way to achieve this, as it can demonstrate the breadth of your reading and your ability to relate your reading to the aims of your research. However, this type of literature review is unlikely to be included in the final version of your PhD thesis as its aim is to show the progress of your research at a particular point in time. It represents your thinking at that moment and recognizes that your thinking may change before the final version has been produced.

An interim literature review is also an opportunity to show how you write. Your supervisors (and perhaps the members of a supervisory board) are unlikely to have seen an example of your extended writing and will be interested to see whether the standard of your writing meets their expectations. So it is perhaps your first real opportunity to show that you can write clearly and concisely at the required level and your first opportunity to try to clarify your stance with respect to your research project. For these reasons, interim literature reviews are standard practice for PhD projects in many disciplinary areas. In some cases they may also be a requirement for upgrading from MPhil to PhD status.

Voice in a literature review

A literature review needs to be more than just a survey of what has been written in a particular area. It must also contain *your own presence* and expose readers to *your own voice*. Dunleavy (1986: 114) refers to this as an 'angle' that readers will have no difficulty in identifying.

When producing a literature review, there is a danger that you can become so absorbed in what other people have to say that your own voice can disappear. There are psychological reasons as well as technical reasons for this. Subconsciously, you may feel somewhat uncomfortable in the company of eminent writers in the field because you believe that your own position must somehow be worth less than theirs. You cannot allow this to happen. You have to be present in any literature review that you produce, and prominently so. What you are conveying to the reader might be summarized as follows: 'I am not reviewing this literature in a neutral way as an impartial observer. I am doing this to explore themes that are relevant to my own research and to test the claims that I intend to put forward.'

Ideally, you will provide at the outset a statement of intent in relation to the perspective (or angle) that you intend to provide. Once identified, your individual approach will inform the selection of source materials that are discussed and the conclusions that you draw from this discussion. An example of how this might work is provided below:

Box 4.2. A literature review introduction

The serialisation of The Age of Innocence did not attract as much interest amongst readers and critics as the later prize-winning publication of the novel. The serialised work was accompanied by two types of visual imagery. The first kind is related to the text and may affect its reading and understanding. The second type comprises advertisements which are of a different format and style, yet its presence certainly interacts with the novel's themes of perpetuating female beauty. The material placed within the text falls under four categories: W. B. King's illustrations, the poems with their drawings, small design elements introducing the text, and editorial statements. My main focus here will be on studying King's illustrations, and the societal implications behind the relationships between the characters portrayed within the context of New York's changing society. I will bring to light how the illustrations provide a new dimension to our understanding of the novel's embedded social, cultural, and economic themes.

Conventions in other disciplinary areas may not allow such a strong statement of intent at the very beginning of a literature review. Where it is a possible option, you should consider it carefully because it makes clear to the reader the nature of your individual approach.

Other suggestions that may help you make your voice heard include the following:

- exploring relevant projects and case studies in research contexts that are comparable to your own
- testing the specific research questions that you have formulated against what is in the literature: 'Who has asked these questions before? With what results?'
- examining the claims you have formulated and testing them, also considering counterclaims and how they can be refuted
- justifying your research methodology in relation to other studies in the literature

How will your literature review be structured?

As a first step, Hart (1998: 186–7) suggests arranging your literature review notes into three sections. The aims of this exercise are to clarify the purpose of your literature review and then identify a suitable structure:

1. a summary of existing work on the topic area – different approaches, different issues that have emerged, key terms and concepts
2. a critical evaluation of previous work – assessing the 'methodologies and methods that have been employed previously to study the topic and evaluate the relative strengths and weaknesses of the literature'
3. general and specific conclusions about work done to date on the topic – identifying gaps, inconsistencies and contradictions

As far as the structure of the literature review itself is concerned, there are no ready-made solutions. PhD theses in some disciplinary areas (especially in the natural sciences) may not require a lengthy literature review. Meanwhile, in other subject areas the literature review can occupy several chapters or sections of many different chapters. For some writers, there will be a requirement to write a separate literature review that focuses on the research methodology and data collection methods: for others, this kind of discussion can be contained in a short section of an individual chapter.

However, it is possible to provide some general guidelines that will help you to find a suitable structure that is accessible to the reader. (For a more detailed discussion of how to build a clear structure into all PhD thesis chapters, see Chapter 6.)

Adding a **short introductory section** to your literature review can help make the individual approach that you are adopting more accessible to the reader. Explain how your own research questions will influence the content of the review and its structure.

The **definition and exploration of key concepts** will be a necessary element in the early sections of the review. In the arts/humanities and in social science subject areas, most literature-review chapters seek to engage in a debate which involves 'contested concepts' where multiple interpretations are possible. It is important to clarify your own understanding of such concepts from the very beginning to prevent possible miscommunication with your readers. Chapter 5 will discuss in greater detail the issues and the skills involved.

A **thematic organization** provides the structural framework for many literature reviews. Your own research questions or the findings of other writers can help you identify the important themes that need to be explored. Alternative ways of structuring the main body of the literature review might be chronological (providing a descriptive account of the relevant literature), 'problem-solution' (focusing on questions asked by other researchers followed by their findings) or according to theoretical frameworks (comparing different ways of explaining the phenomena that are of interest). See Hart (1998) for further examples of frameworks.

A **short concluding section** will help you pull together the different strands of the debate, summarize your main conclusions and provide a link to the following chapters of your thesis.

▶ **Literature review problem areas**

Two of the most significant problem areas in producing a successful PhD level literature review have been discussed in detail in Chapter 3, namely the difficulty involved in developing suitable *selection criteria for reading* and the importance of *leaving your tracks* to enable you to reconnect with your thinking at some point in the future. It is now worth considering some additional problem areas experienced by PhD writers. Uncertainty concerning these points can severely disrupt the process of engaging with the literature and producing a review that matches the expectations of readers.

Who are the main readers?
This is a source of confusion for many PhD writers. Are you writing for examiners, for supervisory boards that are set up to monitor your progress, for your supervisors or for a wider public? For an interim literature review,

the answer is relatively straightforward – the target readers are most probably the members of a supervisory board.

For the final literature review, the situation is more complex. Clearly, writers following the 'by papers model' of the PhD will aim to publish their work to as wide a readership as possible. They might intend to publish individual research papers or a book that combines these papers on a related theme. For most other writers, the expectation should also be that the thesis will eventually be read by a wider community rather than two PhD examiners. In the first instance, however, the most important readers will be the examiners themselves. As it is unlikely that you will know both external and internal examiners well, you will need to try to put yourself in their position as readers. What will be their main expectations? What problems might they experience when engaging with your completed text? Which aspects of your work will you need to take particular care in explaining? It is worth noting that these are also useful questions to consider when preparing for the final viva.

How much information do you need to provide?

How far should you spell things out? To what extent should you assume knowledge on the part of the reader? This is a sensitive area for many people. Inexperienced research writers can worry that readers will feel patronized if they are provided with information that is already familiar to them. To prevent this from happening, the safe option appears to be to avoid spelling things out and to assume that readers will be at least as knowledgeable as you are.

The consequences of such an approach may be serious if your text becomes less accessible to your reader as a result. It is easy to overestimate what your readers know and to underestimate your own knowledge in what will become your own specialist area. As a reader, I am not usually offended by being asked to read something that I already know: if this is not of interest, I can skip to the next section of the text. However, if I cannot understand a series of references because of my own lack of knowledge, I will have no means of addressing this gap unless I seek outside solutions.

This approach makes another assumption that is worth contesting, namely that examiners and other readers give equal merit to every word and every sentence of your text. This is not the case. Examiners are experienced writers and readers, who may have a preferred method of engaging with a text. Examiner A might decide not to start at the beginning of your work but go straight to the results or the conclusions. Earlier sections of your text may be skipped through quickly if this type of reader recognizes familiar territory. Whereas Examiner B may think 'I do not know this area particularly well.

I will need to read this background information quite carefully' and read your chapters in their intended order, paying equal attention to all of them.

It is perhaps natural to worry about treating our readers as unintelligent beings who need to have everything explained. Luckily, there are some practical solutions available to you:

1. *Provide explicit signposts in the text* that state explicitly that you intend to make a short digression to explain your ideas more carefully. The reader who has no need of the digression will skip the section and go on.
2. Make use of *footnotes*, provided that disciplinary conventions allow this. As footnotes are separate from the text, they provide a suitable means of including information that some readers will need while others will not.
3. Make use of *appendices* as a source of reference. You can provide a more detailed explanation for some readers in an appendix and refer to it.
4. If you are uncertain how much information to include, remember the old maxim: When in doubt, spell it out.

How can you be knowledgeable and avoid being derivative?

Literature reviews are strong if the writer is very knowledgeable. But most students start off not knowing a lot, so they are learning while they are reading. So at the beginning you are strongly influenced by what people are saying, but by the end you can discuss things in depth. (1st-year PhD student)

Even when you are beginning to formulate your research questions and to define the parameters of your research, you should have a view. You may believe that it is not a particularly well-formed view and that you may soon go in a different direction, but it still needs to be recorded and to be valued. Later, you may find yourself returning to it. In the meantime, how can you be confident that your point of view can be defended?

A useful approach when planning a literature review is to seek out apparent inconsistencies or ideas which do not seem to have been fully developed or explained by other writers. Whether they appear as small gaps in knowledge or areas of ambiguity, these can be your focus. You will carefully consider the opinions and theories put forward by other writers, and then you will offer your own. In many arts, humanities and social sciences disciplines, writers can exploit 'grey areas' in this way. At a later stage, you may reject what you have written or (to your surprise) may realize that it still retains its value. If you have reason to believe that you can no longer be confident in a particular point of view, then you can change it. No literature review can be expected to act as a definitive statement. Instead, it is useful to consider it as a means of mapping the progress of your thinking.

If you ask your supervisor or any other academic what they think of their first ever published article or piece of writing, you will receive a mixed response. One person may refuse even to provide you with the reference, while another will say: 'When I go back to it, I'm actually quite pleased with it. I think it isn't so bad after all'. Some writers mature slowly, while others provide their best work at the beginning of their careers. The lesson is that you need to be as confident as you can be in your first attempt at formulating your own point of view until evidence shows that you need to revise it.

Task 4.1: Self-evaluation

1. What type of literature review do you need for your PhD thesis?
2. Will you also need to write an interim literature review? What are the requirements for this?
3. Will there be a separate literature review for your research methodology?
4. What steps will you follow to assemble the relevant literature?
5. How will you record what you have read?
6. How will you integrate your reading notes into the literature review?
7. What will be your preferred structure?

Action Points

1. Consider the role of the literature review in your own research project. In consultation with a supervisor, specify your aims.
2. Decide how the literature review will fit into your finished thesis. Will it occupy a single chapter or be spread across chapters? Will you need a separate literature review to support your research design and methodology?
3. Plan and write an interim literature review as your first substantial piece of doctoral level written work.
4. For any kind of literature review, consider how you will include your own voice and make it distinct from the voices of other writers.
5. Consider alternative structures for the final literature review, and select the one that seems appropriate for your project.
6. Carefully craft an introduction to your literature review that will enable your readers to identify your individual approach or 'angle'. Decide how much contextual information needs to be included or excluded within your review. Clearly signpost any contextual digressions.

5 Exploring Key Concepts

> *This chapter*
>
> - *considers the importance of exploring and developing key concepts during the early stages of PhD research*
> - *argues that a mix of lateral and linear thinking is needed to help researchers examine connections between key concepts, thus contributing to the production of new theories*
> - *outlines the main stages in concept exploration and development*
> - *provides guidelines for concept definition and development in writing*

► The importance of concept development within a research project

It is difficult to imagine attempting a literature review of any sort without exploring the key concepts embedded in the research topic, research questions, claims or hypotheses. The reason for this is clear: if you as the writer assume that the reader will understand complex concepts in a certain way, your assumption might be correct or it might be wrong. It is necessary to spell out precisely what it is that you mean by such terms in the particular context in which you are writing. However, this cannot normally be achieved by means of a simple dictionary-type definition. You can attempt to do this, but the chances of failure are high. What needs to be done instead is to carefully unpack and explore the concept in question. The process begins with reading to see if there is agreement concerning the meaning of a particular concept within your field. An examination of the literature in your field may indicate that multiple interpretations are possible. Outside a single disciplinary area, there may be an even greater variety for you to consider.

Your ultimate aim will be to include a section or sections within the literature review or elsewhere in the thesis in which definitions of your key concepts are carefully explored. This is not just a glossary or list of terms where an explanatory sentence or two is added to each item. For certain terms, an entry in a separate glossary may suffice, but for complex key concepts with multiple possible interpretations, something more will be required.

Which concepts will you need to explore and develop most carefully? The answer will become apparent only as your research progresses, but you will certainly need to consider the following in relation to your research:

- concepts that feature prominently in research questions or claims
- concepts that are relatively new or unfamiliar to readers in your field
- concepts that appear to be unstable or fluid
- concepts that appear to be contested by certain writers

Concept fluidity

Before discussing the steps involved in the exploration of key concepts, it is useful to consider a few examples that will illustrate the potential for instability or fluidity in meanings. Where dictionary definitions are provided, they are taken from the *Collins English Dictionary* (See Appendix 1).

Intelligence: 'the capacity for understanding; ability to perceive and comprehend meaning; good mental capacity'.

If you start adding some extra elements to this particular concept, the range of its possible meanings can become more complex. A good example has been provided by Goleman (1996), who questions the assumption that the term 'intelligence' must necessarily refer to cognitive processes and abilities. A new concept, that of 'emotional intelligence' was created along with a series of theories related to the concept. Goleman argues that what he calls emotional intelligence is an important human attribute, enabling a person to relate to other people, to relate to social situations and above all to cope with the psychological effects of failure. Thus the concept of 'intelligence' has been extended by one writer in an unexpected direction. Other writers have followed Goleman's example with the result that there is now a shared understanding of it. Acceptance is, however, not unanimous: the concept remains contested.

Autonomy: 'the right or state of self-government; freedom to determine one's own actions or behaviours'.

The dictionary indicates that this concept is a familiar one in a political context (*autonomous states, autonomous republics*) and its meaning closely aligns with that of 'self-governance'. In other contexts, however, it appears to have slightly different connotations when certain additions are made. In education, 'learner autonomy' is an example of a contested concept which is sometimes contrasted with 'learner independence'. For some writers in the field, the two terms are interchangeable, while for others there is a clear distinction between the two. Benson and Voller (1997) have produced a book on this subject, the first chapter of which is devoted to a discussion on why there is so much disagreement concerning these two concepts (or single concept, depending on your point of view).

Tradition: 'the handing down from generation to generation of the same customs, beliefs; a specific custom or practice of long standing'.

The concept seems to be neutral at first glance, but once it is altered slightly and the adjectival form 'traditional' is used, it can be contrasted with 'modern' and a pejorative meaning emerges. As soon as we begin to manipulate such concepts, their fluidity and ability to change meaning become apparent. It is clearly a useful step to consider both *concept pairs* (autonomy vs independence) and *derived forms* (tradition vs traditional). In the case of pairs, we sometimes find that a clear distinction is generally accepted and agreed on, as in the final example:

Tax avoidance vs tax evasion: 'reduction or minimization of tax liability by lawful methods' vs 'reduction or minimization of tax liability by illegal methods'.

Here, there is a clearly defined difference in meaning. The former is seen to be perfectly legal (though arguably immoral), while the latter is illegal because it involves deliberate falsification of information. It appears that two common words ('avoidance' and 'evasion'), often used interchangeably without the addition of 'tax', have evolved recognizably distinct meanings when the 'tax' label is added.

▶ The starting point for concept exploration

We can begin to explore concepts *based on our own experience or intuitive understanding*, but this is likely to be problematic, as demonstrated in the examples given below. Another possible approach (as discussed above) might be to rely on *dictionary definitions*. These, however, are likely to be insufficient for our purposes except in the case of technical concepts with a clearly defined single meaning agreed on by all. In the arts, humanities and social sciences, such concepts are comparatively rare.

Before committing yourself to a particular definition of a concept, you will need to consider all the alternatives. Consider for example, these initial attempts by a group of PhD students at defining two concepts that are supposedly related – 'cooperation' and 'altruism'.

Box 5.1. Definition of 'cooperation'

Cooperation is a broad category that refers to any interaction or joint action for a common purpose or goal. Cooperation is pervasive in the natural world, as well as in human society. It usually involves reciprocity and common benefits, but it can also involve (and it often does involve) altruism.

In any such definition, you will need to question and even challenge the assumptions that appear to be built into each of its component parts. In this case, there seem to be two assumptions.

Assumption 1: 'cooperation is always for a common purpose or goal'

This is not difficult to challenge. Consider, for example, political alliances where countries decide to cooperate with each other. It is possible that their goals might be shared (for example, to defeat a common enemy); it is equally likely, however, that they may have completely different agendas.

Assumption 2: 'cooperation usually involves reciprocity'

This is less easy to challenge, but also debatable. There is no evidence to suggest that cooperation is shared more or less equally by two cooperating partners. In the case of forced cooperation, it is arguable that one partner is more likely to demonstrate active cooperative behaviour. Such problems extend to the definition of the supposedly related concept of 'altruism':

Box 5.2. Definition of 'altruism'

There is a remarkable lack of precise agreement over what is meant by the term. It is often used interchangeably with giving, sharing, cooperating, helping and different forms of other-directed and prosocial behaviour. But in general, altruism could be defined as a particular form of cooperative behaviour for the benefit of another, and which might involve some form of sacrifice to the altruist.

The concept of altruism is notoriously difficult to explore. Arguably, it may not exist in a pure form, since the altruist will usually gain some credit or benefits for his/her actions. It is also possible that the reputational gain experienced by the 'altruist' may sometimes outweigh the material gain of the receiver of an altruistic act. The reputation of the biblical Good Samaritan remains while the details of his good deeds may be forgotten.

Consider also intuitive interpretations of three other problematic concepts and the supposed relationship between them: *'values'*, *'beliefs'* and *'attitudes'*. An intuitive understanding might place 'values' at the deepest level. One example could be embedded and shared 'cultural values' which may not even be apparent at a conscious level. These in turn might influence the formulation of 'beliefs' nurtured by individuals. Such beliefs can then manifest themselves as 'attitudes', which in turn can inform 'behaviour'.

One way to test this supposed relationship might be to conduct an 'images' Internet search. In this particular case, there are diagrams readily available that provide a visual representation of the relationship between these concepts. However, it soon becomes evident that some of these present a different interpretation, with 'beliefs' leading to 'values' rather than the other way round. See Appendix 1 for one example.

Considering alternative representations of the relationship between concepts can produce examples such as these. The next step might be to produce a simplified diagram to summarize your own views at this stage of your exploration:

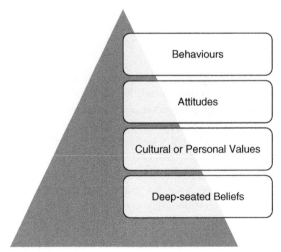

Fig 5.1 A concept pyramid

Other ways of beginning the process of concept exploration might include

- starting with a *definition provided by a well-known writer* in a seminal text. This could begin a debate in which you can present the points of view of other writers

- *considering concepts in pairs or in groups*, where you can begin to see meanings in relation to interpretations of related concepts. Examples already given in this chapter include 'tax avoidance' vs 'tax evasion' and 'independence' compared to 'autonomy'
- *breaking down different meanings* either *by additions* (for example 'learner' added to 'autonomy', 'emotional' added to 'intelligence', 'liberal' added to 'democracy') or *by changing the form of the concept itself* ('traditional' considered alongside 'tradition', 'modernism' when compared to 'modern')

▶ The process of concept exploration: the next steps

When a concept such as 'altruism' is carefully examined, we begin to realize how fluid it is in terms of its ability to change meaning when transposed from one specific context to another. Building credit for oneself by means of altruistic acts in (for example) the context of religious beliefs and practices can seem the exact opposite of an intuitive understanding of altruism itself.

A definition of such a difficult concept would have to be reached at the end of a process of exploration rather than at the beginning. In between, it is necessary to work slowly and carefully through the following steps:

1. Understand the different interpretations of key terms through your reading.
2. Clarify different meanings and interpretations in your notes.
3. Communicate these meanings to others through your writing so that you can share your chosen interpretation and at the same time justify it.

This process has to begin in the early stages of PhD work. It is essential that you clarify meanings in your own mind before you begin to use key concepts as part of theory construction. As suggested by Dunleavy (1986), it is difficult to achieve this only in a linear way: 'lateral' or nonlinear thinking is also required. Lateral thinking, popularized by De Bono (1970), allows you to make new associations between concepts that seem familiar but can be subjected to questioning to reveal the assumptions that underlie them. The idea is that we begin to see these concepts and the connections between them in a different way: this enables us to make new connections and to construct new theories on the basis of which claims can be formulated.

To illustrate the importance of examining the relation between concepts as part of theory construction and to see how this can work powerfully in practice, consider a traditional puzzle that I learnt at school over 50 years ago (origin unknown):

Box 5.3. Lateral thinking puzzle 1

A woman walks into a bar and asks for a glass of water. The barman pulls out a gun and points it at her. The woman thanks him and leaves.

How can this series of apparently illogical events be explained so that it makes sense? A number of different theories may be possible. To enable us to construct them, we will need to ask questions such as:

- Why does this woman want a glass of water?
- Why does the barman respond by pulling out a gun?
- Why does the woman thank him?

To find alternative answers to our questions, concepts such as 'bar', 'glass of water', 'gun', 'barman', 'thank' will need to be carefully examined by asking more detailed questions:

- Is the gun real? Or a toy gun?
- Is this really a bar or has the unfortunate woman lost her way?
- Do the woman and the barman know each other well enough to play a practical joke of some kind on each other?

By trial and error, we may be able to create a number of theories that will account for the sequence of events and connect them together logically by means of some lateral thinking. Here are some possibilities:

1. The gun is in fact a water pistol which the barman squirts at the woman.
2. The barman pulls out a special kind of gun that dispenses soft drinks, points it at her and asks if she would like a glass.
3. The woman has hiccups and believes that drinking water will cure them. The barman decides to frighten her by pointing the gun. This works equally well.

The 'correct answer' to the puzzle is, of course, theory 3. However, the others have certain merits in providing a meaningful interpretation of the events. The point to recognize is that on the surface the events cannot make sense if we make the most reasonably intuitive assumptions available (for example, believing that she asks for water because she is thirsty or that the barman pulls out a gun in order to threaten her). Lateral thinking enables us to try out alternative explanations by re-examining such assumptions and the connections between the different events.

Here is another puzzle for you to try out:

Box 5.4. Lateral thinking puzzle 2

In the middle of the night, a man picks up a telephone and dials a number. As soon as someone answers, he smiles and hangs up.

How can you explain this series of events? Questions to ask might include:

- Why does the man make a phone call in the middle of the night?
- Why does he smile and hang up as soon as someone answers?

Try out different theories that will adequately explain the sequence of events.

Lateral thinking can also be applied to reading where, as noted in Chapter 3, we often attempt to detect inconsistencies or flaws in argumentation, missing pieces of evidence or evidence that appears to be contradictory. Thinking laterally will allow us to consider other theories that might be generated using the same evidence ('what if ...').

For many people the problem of engaging in lateral thinking exercises is simple: it requires the suspension of linear thinking. Smart (2013: 12) in *Autopilot: The Art and Science of Doing Nothing* argues that nonlinearity is an essential function of the brain, but one that we systematically repress by engaging in too much planned mental activity:

> *Allowing the brain to rest opens the system to exploiting these mechanisms of nonlinearity and randomness, and amplifies the brain's natural tendency to combine percepts and memories into new concepts. Anecdotal evidence from writers and artists, as well as recent psychological studies, leads to the understanding that in order to really tap the creative potential of the brain, a complex nonlinear system, we should allow ourselves long, uninterrupted periods of idleness.*

The premise of Smart's book is that mental activity actually increases during periods of apparent idleness. In order to allow lateral thinking techniques to have an effect, linear thinking will need to be temporarily suspended.

For further practice in exploiting the nonlinearity of the brain, I recommend lateral thinking puzzles and exercises presented in quiz programmes such as the BBC's *Only Connect* (see Appendix 1). In this programme, an exercise entitled 'the wall' requires contestants to find links between different concepts. There are 16 concepts that have to be organized into four sets with distractors that may appear to belong to one set, but if interpreted in a slightly different way belong to another. Sometimes to make an association it is necessary to apply a different kind of logic, as in the following example where the underlined portion of the word would provide a numerical clue:

Weight	Network	Cone	Feminine

Consider also the following, linked together only by the addition of the word 'social':

Security	Services	Media	Issues

Contestants in such programmes demonstrate that it is possible to develop to a high degree the skills required to make such nonlinear connections. For many others, finding lateral connections will be a demanding mental exercise.

▶ Other ways of exploring concepts through lateral thinking

Dunleavy (1986) recommends using other lateral thinking techniques to establish connections, construct new theories and even formulate entirely new concepts.

Finding antonyms

To explore what a concept might mean, one approach could be to consider what it is not. Sometimes this can make clear patterns of meaning that are hard to find in a linear fashion. Thus, in order to explore the range of possible meanings for 'racism', it may be possible to focus on a precise definition by considering what an absence of this concept might mean.

- *Tolerance* would equate 'racism' with 'intolerance'
- *Inclusivity* would imply 'exclusion'
- *Cosmopolitanism* would imply 'parochialism'
- *Broad-mindedness* would imply 'narrow-mindedness'

Placing concepts on a scale

To prevent 'false dichotomies', which may arise from considering opposing concepts, it may be useful to attempt to locate key concepts within a scale or continuum. For example, in the example below it would be interesting to discuss the placement of 'absolute monarchy' and 'constitutional monarchy' on the continuum. The 'end point' concepts would also need to be carefully considered: are they in fact two extremes, or do other concepts need to be added?

DICTATORSHIP   DEMOCRACY

└─────────────┴─────────────┴─────────────┴─────────────┘

Exploring concept associations
Consider these possible additions to 'culture' and the changes that they might bring to the more basic concept:

High culture
Popular culture
Folk culture
Youth culture
National culture
Organizational culture

Exploring concept derivations
Comparing and contrasting slight variations of the phrasing of a particular concept can help clarify the specific context in which each is used. Here is an example:

Nation
Nationality
Nationalism
Nationalist
Internationalism
Nationalization

Examining degrees of separation between different concepts
It can often be useful to examine the exact relationship (in terms of separation) of pairs of concepts which are clearly related in some way. Concepts can be quite separate from each other or can overlap in some way, or one concept can wholly include another. Finally, concepts can be considered identical if there is only one area of meaning to be established.

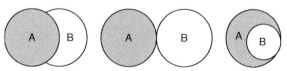

Fig 5.2 Degrees of separation between concepts

Task 5.1: Unpacking concept pairs

How would you describe the relationship between the concepts of 'method' and 'methodology' in a research context? Which of the diagrams in Fig 5.2 (based on those created by Dunleavy (1986)) might best represent this relationship?

▶ Exploring concepts in writing

When concepts are problematic and in particular when they appear to be contested by different writers, a careful written exploration will be required. Within a literature review, it is possible that an entire section may need to be dedicated to concept exploration and subsequent definition. Similarly, in individual research papers an introductory section focusing on key concepts may be required.

An example of 'good practice' in this respect is reproduced below. The key concept in question (the 'speech community') is contested by some authors in the field. The aim of the research paper is to argue the case in favour of this concept:

> *The speech community is the locus of most sociolinguistic and anthropological-linguistic research, indeed all linguistic research that is accountable to a body of naturally-occurring speech or signed data. It represents the social boundaries within which analysts locate, and seek to describe and account for, language variation and change, ways of speaking, and patterns of choice in a linguistic repertoire. It is thus on a par with other basic notions such as 'language', 'dialect' or 'grammar' as a primary object of description and theorizing in our discipline. Like these notions, it is both central and elusive, with definitions frequently offered and even more often called into question – one of those ideas linguists cannot agree on amongst ourselves, and appear to remain happily ambivalent about, while referring to it in textbooks and introductory lectures as though its nature were quite well understood.* (Patrick 1998)

After this basic definition, the author guides us through the development of the concept by means of the following steps:

* origins of the concept
* how the concept has developed over time
* a key definition from a well-known author in the field
* reactions to this definition (both extreme and more moderate)
* the author's definition in response to all of the above

Concept development in written text requires a clear structure and direction. A step-by-step approach towards establishing a preferred definition guides the reader and helps justify the author's perspective. Over a period of time academic writers can fully develop their analysis of contested concepts, as has happened in this particular case. See, for example, Patrick (2002: 573–97) for a more extensive treatment of the concept leading to the conclusion that it still remains 'fraught with difficulties'.

For further consideration of different ways in which concepts may be developed in writing, we return to the Nelson and Lamboll 2012 text on 'Climate Change' briefly discussed in Chapter 3. The aim of this paper is to establish relationships between 'Climate Change', 'Agriculture' and 'Development', three problematic concepts that will need to be explored in a number of ways. Two examples are a consideration of 'sustainable' versus 'non-sustainable agriculture', and 'mitigation' versus 'adaptation strategies' for dealing with climate change.

One interesting aspect of the paper is that it presents three distinct *modes* of concept exploration:

1. continuous text
2. a diagram linking three key concepts laterally
3. a table which summarizes and compares sample definitions of key concepts

Finally, in addition to individual texts which can present models of 'good practice', there are some readily available sources of inspiration for struggling writers in the form of 'concept development' guides. These generally consist of short essays which aim to explore concepts that resist straightforward definition. Usually, they relate to interpretations of concepts in one specific disciplinary area. Occasionally, however, they span several related fields of study.

Perhaps the best-known example of the latter category is Raymond Williams' 'Keywords', first published in 1976. In his introduction to the book, Williams described his experiences of returning to Britain from army service and discovering changes in attitudes that seemed to result in changes in the way language was used to express ideas. In particular, the different interpretations of the word 'culture' interested him. He noted that he had previously understood the concept in two ways, either as 'the preferred word for a kind of social superiority' or as an overall descriptive label that referred to the creation and appreciation of novels, poetry, plays and paintings. However, new uses of the word appeared to be emerging, most notably the idea of culture as 'a particular way of life'.

Williams recognized the fluidity of such broad concepts and decided to analyse their development through *Keywords*. In the entry for 'culture' he guides us through the agricultural origins of the word to more recent interpretations. This process of unpacking meanings is repeated for other concepts, including 'art', society', 'history', 'management' and more than one hundred others.

There is now a huge range of similar 'concept guides' available as works of reference. Such sources can be a useful support for concept exploration, but they are not intended as a substitute for thinking or meant to be pasted into a text as pieces of ready-made analysis. Instead, they can help to broaden your interpretations of concepts that are central to your own research and perhaps even show the way towards the development of new variants.

Action Points

1. Identify the key concepts that you will need to explore as part of your research.
2. Begin the process of exploration by comparing and contrasting them with similar concepts. To what extent do meanings overlap?
3. Avoid intuitive or dictionary-type definitions of key concepts at the beginning of the process of exploration.
4. Single out any contested concepts for more careful consideration.
5. Use lateral thinking techniques to establish new or unfamiliar connections between key concepts.
6. Within a literature review, prepare a structured exploration of the key concepts that readers will need to understand. Justify your own interpretation through carefully considered arguments.

6 Building a Structured Chapter Framework

This chapter

- *considers the importance of the table of contents and the abstract as tools for mapping out the structure of a doctoral thesis*
- *argues that a clear structure is also dependent on the formulation of chapter and chapter section headings and subheadings*
- *explores the role of signposting devices that guide the reader, making the text more accessible*
- *examines the characteristics of different types of chapters within a thesis*
- *considers the need for well-crafted introductory and concluding sections within individual thesis chapters*

► Producing an overall framework

The table of contents and abstract

At a certain point during the first year of research, it is likely that your general approach to writing will begin to change. Developing the research topic, managing reading and generating research questions will gradually give way to a consideration of what the written end product is going to look like. You will start thinking in terms of chapters, and you will begin to consider your readers and their expectations.

PhD supervisors often ask for a rough overview of intended chapters during the early stages, but your initial reaction may be that you do not feel ready to provide this. There are understandable reasons for this reaction. Before you can define the end product, you will first need to consider the scope and the parameters of your research: however, at this stage you may have more questions than answers in this respect. Whatever you do in terms of trying to plan your writing, you will need to be aware that your thinking and therefore your planning will inevitably change as your research progresses.

Before you begin to plan your writing, you will also need to think in very general terms about the task that lies ahead. It is possible that this could be the longest piece of writing that you will ever attempt, and one key area of difficulty is the requirement for overall coherence. You will need to develop arguments that readers can follow without getting lost throughout a lengthy text. Meanwhile, you will also need to prevent yourself from losing your way as you gradually and painstakingly construct this text. Ensuring that coherence is maintained will eventually be achieved in different ways (some of which will be discussed in detail in Chapter 8). At this initial stage of chapter writing, the first step will be to focus on a draft *structural framework*.

Such a framework will need to help you 'manage the expectations of readers', in the words of Dunleavy (2003). It will be necessary to consider disciplinary writing conventions, what is expected or proscribed and whether you are going to satisfy those expectations. If you decide that you need to ignore or contravene conventions in any way, you will need to provide clear explanations or justifications to readers whose expectations are not being met. For example, if your readers expect a designated methodology chapter and your thesis structure does not contain one, you will need to manage this situation carefully.

A *clear table of contents* is the first means of achieving structural clarity. Tables of contents create expectations in readers' minds, which the sections of your chapters then need to match. If you write a table of contents which does not seem entirely relevant to the finished text, readers may become frustrated. Before they start to look at your work in detail, they will consult your table of contents in the expectation that it will provide a clear map of what they are about to read. An example of a first attempt at a table of contents is given below.

Box 6.1 A first draft table of contents

Buddhist minorities in India: a Human Rights perspective and its legal implications

Chapter 1: Introduction

1.1. Wider context
1.2. The analytical framework
1.3. Main aims of this thesis
1.4. The structure
1.5. Caveats

→

Chapter 2: Human Rights Perspective

2.1. Definition of 'minorities'
2.2. Buddhist minorities in India – a postmodern existence
2.3. Significance of their existence
2.4. Right against discrimination
2.5. Right to profess and practise one's own religion
2.6. Concoction and camouflaging of the religious sites

Chapter 3: Case Study – the Bodhgaya Temple

3.1. Introduction
3.2. History and importance of the Bodhgaya Temple
3.3. The Bodhgaya Temple Management Act 1949
3.4. Violation of articles 25 and 26 of the Constitution of India
3.5. Struggle for its emancipation

Chapter 4: Historical Background

4.1. Historicity of India
4.2. The terms 'Hindu' and 'Hinduism'
4.3. Pre-eminence of Buddhism prior to the advent of Muslims in India
4.4. When, why and how Buddhism disappeared in India
4.5. Co-option of Buddhism into Brahmanism
4.6. Rediscovery of Buddhism by the British
4.7. Concerns of minorities during the British Raj
4.8. Buddhism in South Asia
4.9. Revival of Buddhism in India
4.10. Present state

Chapter 5: Constitutional and Legislative Issues

5.1. Development of Constitutional Law in India vis-à-vis the minorities
5.2. Issues of minorities and the Constituent Assembly Debates
5.3. Article 25 of the Constitution of India
5.4. Reflection of Article 25 in other legislative instruments
5.5. The Hindu code and its 'Hindu' hegemony
5.6. Debates regarding the 'Application of Acts' of the Hindu Code
5.7. Legal pluralism and informality
5.8. Issue of Uniform Civil Code

Chapter 6: Judicial Interpretation and Institutional Responses

6.1. Case-laws on the term 'Hindu' and on article 25 of the Constitution of India
6.2. Case-laws on the issues of Buddhist minorities
6.3. Juristic writings

→

6.4. Overlapping vagueness in between 'Reconstruction' and 'Deconstruction'
6.5. Executive actions
6.6. Issue of reservations
6.7. Media
6.8. Voluntary organizations
6.9. Academia and experts
6.10. Religious institutions
6.11. International concerns

Chapter 7: Problems within the Community

7.1. Vulnerable existence
7.2. Undeveloped rituals and religious practices
7.3. Search of alternative roots
7.4. Status gained in sociocultural perspective
7.5. Lack of cohesion within the community

Chapter 8: Conclusion

8.1. Identity, status and existence: claimed and gained
8.2. Vulnerability during transition

Overall, this has to be considered a worthy first attempt to structure chapters which have yet to be written. The writer appears to have a clear idea of the structure of later chapters as well as earlier chapters of the thesis, which is unusual. Arguably, however, the draft structure contains several features that will seem unexpected or ambiguous to a reader:

1. The order of chapters seems counterintuitive with the 'historical background' chapter placed in the middle of the structure rather than at the beginning.
2. Readers might also reasonably expect the Chapter 3 case study to come later in the sequence after the chapters which appear to be more theoretical.
3. There is no mention of research methodology or data collection methods in the structure. While 'methodology' might not merit a whole chapter, there is a reasonable expectation that a chapter section might be given this label.
4. There are apparent sources of ambiguity in chapter section labels.
5. A new concept, 'vulnerability during transition', appears for the first time in the last chapter.

Questions or criticisms should be expected after your first attempt. This is work in progress, with your structure likely to be modified many times before reaching its finalized version.

Although the formulation of a chapter framework may seem premature during the early stages of research, there is another useful purpose for creating it. A draft table of contents such as this one can act as a useful mediation document between yourself, your supervisors and other potential readers. The type of feedback points listed above could provide a significant means of helping you clarify your own thinking. A draft table of contents is a useful document both for your readers and yourself – the end product of an important writing exercise which needs to take place during the early stages of your research.

Producing a first version of your *research abstract* to accompany the table of contents is also a useful goal. Below is one part of an abstract produced by the writer of the sample table of contents:

Box 6.2. A first draft abstract

Buddhist minorities in India: a Human Rights perspective and its legal implications

This thesis aims to investigate and explore the vulnerable identity, status and existence of the Buddhist minorities in India, which have been consistently subjected to the tendencies of subsumption by the 'majority', on the pretext of constructed legal uniformities and in the guise of misinterpreted mythic historical argumentations. The majority itself was largely oligarchic in its character until recent times and continues to remain stratified; thereby it does not subscribe to the true and well-informed responses of all its components. It is argued that the state of reality vis-à-vis the identity, status and existence of the Buddhist minorities should not be subservient to an all-embracing and precarious entity termed as 'Hindu'.

The central questions to be answered by the current research are: when, why and how were the identity and status of the Buddhist minorities incorporated into the Indian legal framework, and how is that 'process' undermining their existence in terms of human rights principles?

The final version of your abstract will be an important document. It is the gateway to your research, the first piece of your writing that readers are likely to see. Potential readers may decide on the basis of the abstract whether they will read your thesis or not.

A first draft abstract acts as a rationale for your research. As in the above example, it will normally specify research aims or focus and the main research questions. It could also include an outline of your methodology and a consideration of the significance of your research. You will need to write multiple versions of the abstract, updating it as your research progresses. Like the table of contents, it can provide a useful point of reference to help focus discussions with supervisors and other potential readers of your thesis.

For the final version of the abstract, Hartley (2010) provides a useful set of guidelines concerning what might be included. These can be summarized as follows:

- *Background:* outline the issues that led you to work on the topic and explain briefly why you think your research focus has significance for your intended readers
- *Aims:* outline what you set out to achieve
- *Methods/procedures:* describe how you set about to achieve your research aims through the design of your data collection and analysis tools and procedures
- *Results:* report the main findings of the research
- *Conclusions/implications:* summarize your main conclusions and (perhaps) provide suggestions for further research that would extend the work

Organizing the structural framework
In this section, we will discuss the organization of the structural framework of your thesis into its table of contents. The hierarchy of ideas can usually be represented as follows:

Box 6.3. Structural framework hierarchy

THESIS TITLE

CHAPTER TITLE

SECTION/SUBSECTION HEADINGS

TOPIC SENTENCES WITHIN EACH PARAGRAPH

The thesis title provides an overarching description of the research project and will include at least some of its key concepts and themes. Chapter titles, section headings and subsection headings break this down further in a clear and logical manner. Finally, topic sentences (see Chapter 10) signal the content of individual paragraphs. This is the skeleton structure of your thesis. Each level of the hierarchy provides important signposts to enable readers to understand the way in which your ideas will be organized.

There are certain disciplinary conventions which require you to think about the way in which you present your framework. For example, readers of many humanities PhD theses will not expect sections and subsections to be numbered. In contrast, many science disciplines and social science disciplines such as economics do encourage hierarchical structures broken down with several levels of numbers. (*3.1*, *3.1.1*, even *3.1.1.1* in some cases). If your readers expect a numerical breakdown, you will need to justify not meeting their expectations. For cross-disciplinary projects there can be real problems in situations where two sets of conventions clash. Managing reader expectations is even more important here.

At this point it may be useful to present some principles for organizing your structural framework to meet reader expectations:

1. The <u>number of chapters</u> is important. If expectations are for six to eight chapters, you will need to justify a structure which contains more or fewer.
2. The <u>sequence of chapters</u> is important. This should conform to expected norms of logical development within your field or associated fields of study.
3. The <u>overall structure</u> should as far as possible keep the argument on track.
4. <u>Headings for chapters</u> must be clear and informative.

Each of these will be discussed in turn in the sections that follow.

How many chapters should you write?

Although in some disciplines nine or ten chapters might be considered excessive, you will find that it is not difficult to come close to this number as your work progresses. The final structure of my own PhD thesis had nine chapters, even though I had initially anticipated writing six. In fact, ten chapters each containing 8,000 words does not seem unreasonable for a PhD thesis of 80,000 words. However, it is likely that your most important chapters will be longer, perhaps up to 15,000 words. Six to eight chapters might therefore be considered the norm with the introduction and conclusion being counted within this total.

In some cases, the number of chapters may be prescribed. PhD researchers in many science disciplines make use of *LaTex* software (see Appendix 1): this contains templates that suggest the number of chapters to be written and organizes your thesis table of contents for you. In the end, the number of chapters will be a decision that you have to make together with your supervisor. More than nine chapters is perhaps unlikely, while fewer than five would also be unexpected.

Chapter sequencing and structure

If we return to the sample table of contents presented previously, one of the most surprising features was the fact that the 'historical background' chapter appeared after the 'case study' chapter. The explanation for this was interesting: one of the writer's main concerns when constructing his framework was to make sure that the importance of the case study was highlighted. He therefore decided to place the case study chapter earlier in the sequence of chapters than would normally be expected. To achieve this, he was forced to move some of the background chapters (including 'historical background') until later in the sequence.

In later versions of his framework, he decided (rightly) to reverse this decision. The problem here is one of reader expectations and the possible response of readers when meeting a sequence of chapters that seems unjustified. If readers follow the sequence suggested in the first draft, they may be placed in a position where they are forced to engage with the details of a case study for which they may not have the requisite background knowledge. The solution for chapter sequencing is to follow the expected order as far as possible, making radical changes only if you can justify these to both yourself and your readers.

Keeping the argument on track

In any framework, too many sections and too many headings can lead to problems of comprehension as different pieces of text become disconnected from each other. This may have particular relevance for the 'papers' model of PhD thesis, where separate literature reviews and 'methods sections' are often a requirement. However, under-organization of the structural framework may prove to be equally problematic. Too much continuous text without any breaks may result in readers' losing the thread of the argumentation and sense of coherence within the text. Such issues will be discussed in further detail in Chapter 8.

To achieve a good organizational balance, it may help you to work with *two versions* of your table of contents. The first can be much more detailed and is for your own reference, acting as a guide as you slowly build your text.

The other will be the simpler version for the reader, containing less detail and published in the final version of your thesis.

Wording of headings

Chapter and chapter section headings can be problematic when they are:

1. expressed in *non-specific, vague or ambiguous* language so that the reader cannot understand the content of the section that has been labelled
2. *inaccurate*, misleading the reader
3. *repetitive*, making different sections appear alike when they may be very different in terms of their content
4. *inconsistent* in their use of key terminology. From the example provided, if the agreed term is 'evolution', we will need to be careful changing to 'transition' unless there are good reasons
5. *frivolous or flippant*, added to achieve a humorous effect. Humour in PhD theses is certainly not proscribed. It is difficult, however, to create humorous labels which are also substantive and accurate

Certain types of headings may be considered unacceptable in specific disciplines but welcomed in others. For instance, *interrogative headings* are sometimes rejected on stylistic grounds. If they are acceptable to your readers, they can act as a useful structural device, allowing chapters and chapter sections to be organized as an answer to a specific question. However, one potential problem needs to be recognized: it may be that by asking a question in a title, there is an implication that you are about to answer it. If this turns out not to be the case, your readers' expectations will be frustrated.

▶ Types of chapters within the structural framework

In this section, we examine the types of chapters that you will need to consider placing within the structural framework of a 'traditional' PhD thesis. It should be noted that the 'by papers' model of the PhD will require a very different structure with three or four publishable papers linked together by strong introductory and concluding sections.

The short descriptions of typical chapters are intended only as a rough guide to help you fit together the pieces of your own structural framework. It is evident that there will be great variation both across and within disciplines concerning the role of each element. In some cases, the arrangement and balance of chapter content will be prescribed by your readers, while in others you will be allowed more freedom to develop a structure that will fit the needs of your individual research project.

The introductory chapter

This is where you will need to convince readers that what you have to say will be of interest and of significance. There is no requirement to lay out everything on the table at the same time. Instead, your introduction is more likely to select and highlight the most significant aspects of your research. The analogy of a shop window is perhaps more pertinent than that of a market stall.

An introductory chapter can be short, about five to six pages, or much longer if the aim is to present a more detailed research context or provide an explanation of the research methodology. If there is to be no designated methodology chapter, it is often the case that the research design and data collection methods will be presented as part of the introduction.

A useful question to consider is precisely when an introductory chapter should be written. Some supervisors will strongly advise leaving this until the very end. In some ways this makes good sense: if you write the introduction first, as a prediction of where your research might lead, you will probably be forced to rewrite it once your findings have emerged. However, if you delay writing a first draft of your introduction, you will be depriving yourself of a helpful statement of intent that can inform the rest of your work. A useful compromise may be to write at least one draft of an introductory chapter but to keep it for your own reference as a writing guide.

Literature review

Most PhD theses will contain a literature review in some form. A key structural decision is whether there will be one designated chapter that contains the review. Alternatively, the review of the relevant literature may be spread throughout the thesis, built into different chapters. In some cases, there may even be a separate dedicated literature review which focuses on the design of the research and its data collection methods. See Chapter 4 for a full discussion of how literature review chapters can be developed and organized. See Chapter 5 for a discussion of key concept development within a literature review chapter or chapters.

Methodology

According to Walshaw (2012: 124), the purpose of a 'methodology' or 'research design' chapter is:

> to describe what you have done in your study and to provide a justification for the choices made, offering sound reasons for not choosing other options to address your research questions. Your decisions should be explained in such a way that another researcher is absolutely clear about the assumptions underpinning those decisions and would be able to replicate the study.

This type of approach would perhaps be more suited to certain science disciplines, where procedures need to be carefully described, explained and justified. Designated 'research design' chapters are often a requirement in such subject areas. This may also be the case in some non-science disciplines or wherever there is a need to describe in detail and justify how experiments are set up. The approach may be less applicable for arts, humanities and social science subject areas, where it is often a personal choice whether or not to include a separate 'methodology chapter' in the structural framework.

A methodology chapter may also provide an exploration of a particular research model that you have chosen to adopt, especially in cases where the model contravenes disciplinary expectations. A good example was provided by a researcher from the University of London, School of Pharmacy who I once taught. His main research interest was in exploring patients' resistance to taking medicine prescribed for high blood pressure. He decided to conduct a series of semi-structured interviews and focus groups that would yield qualitative data, an approach considered unusual within his discipline. The methodology chapter in his case provided an important justification for his entire research project.

Reporting and analysing findings

Even at an early stage of PhD thesis writing, it is advisable to start thinking ahead to a possible structure for the chapters in which you intend to report and analyse your research data. Questions to consider include the following:

- How will you communicate your results?
- Will your reporting be organized in relation to your research questions?
- Will the findings from each data collection method be reported separately?
- Alternatively, will you structure your data reporting according to certain predetermined or emergent themes?
- Do you intend to tell a story followed by analysis?
- Alternatively, will you build analysis into a reporting narrative?

The answers to such questions will be discussed in detail in Chapter 12.

Conclusion chapters

A conclusion chapter addresses a series of related questions: 'Having examined my key findings in some detail, what does all this mean? What are the implications of what has been discovered? What is their significance for the wider research community? What further studies need to be carried out?' All of these might be summarized in two words: 'So what?'

In your conclusion chapter, you may wish to begin by providing a summary of your findings, but your task does not end there. This chapter provides you with the opportunity to move the discussion beyond the narrow confines of your research project to consider its significance within (and perhaps beyond) your disciplinary area. You may also decide to link back to the literature discussed in earlier chapters and consider whether there is a need to reappraise the way these particular issues have been treated in the past. Finally, the chapter provides you with an opportunity to consider the limitations of your study and to issue an invitation to other researchers to carry on at the point where you have stopped.

Chapters within broader sections

In addition to individual chapters, you may wish to consider grouping chapters into thematically organized sections within your table of contents, as below:

Box 6.4. Examples of thesis sections

Section A: (Chapters 1–2) Research context
Section B: (Chapters 3–4) Research methodology and analytical frameworks
Section C: (Chapters 5–8) Data reporting and analysis

Some writers choose this type of structural framework because they would like to conduct a more theoretical discussion in the early sections of the thesis and to report on an empirical study in the final section. There are advantages in this approach if you are planning to submit sections of your work for publication. The disadvantage in certain subject areas, such as education or medicine, is that you may inadvertently create too great a divide between theoretical considerations and those related to actual practice.

▶ Chapter introductions and conclusions

Crafting chapter introductions

When readers begin a thesis chapter, they will expect to receive some indication of the direction in which the arguments will lead them. If the beginning of a chapter constitutes point A, they will appreciate some indication of the end point of the chapter (point B) and a clearly mapped route between the two. Carefully planned chapter introductions are important for many reasons:

- They help identify the main themes that will be considered in the text.
- They answer the question, 'what function does this chapter serve?' within the thesis' structural framework.
- They make a significant contribution to the overall coherence of the chapter.
- They can map the structure of the rest of the chapter for the reader.
- From the writer's point of view, they also provide a useful map for the rest of the text.
- They can attract the interest of the reader and provide some degree of motivation to engage with the text.
- They can provide a clear indication of how a particular chapter relates to the rest of the thesis. If there are links with other chapters, these can be made explicit, thus contributing to the coherence of the whole text.

There are many different ways of planning the beginning of a chapter, including the following:

a) Referring back to a previous chapter or chapters

> *'In Chapter 3, the connections between X and Y were carefully examined ...'*

This can help readers connect to other relevant parts of your text. You cannot always assume that readers, including examiners, will read your thesis according to the chapter order that you have carefully laid out. Some will prefer to move around within the text and may even begin by reading the reporting of your findings or your conclusions. This kind of opening sentence will indicate to such readers that they may need to refer back to what has been written previously.

Referring back to previous chapters may not provide a particularly memorable opening to a new chapter. However, readers often find this kind of backward referencing to be useful to guide them through the intricacies of a long text. Whether this reference is in the first sentence or the first paragraph is a stylistic issue. I would argue that in a first draft, stylistic issues should not be your primary consideration, though they should not be ignored. If you wish to communicate effectively with readers, considerations of clarity and coherence need to outweigh the need or desire to be stylish. More careful attention to issues of style can always be provided at the editing stage.

b) Direct thesis statements

    'In this chapter, I will argue that ...'

This type of opening has the advantage of coming straight to the point, making clear to the reader both the scope of the chapter and your own position. Establishing your own point of view as early as possible means that clarity and coherence within the chapter will be easier to establish and maintain.

The main disadvantage of getting to the point in the very first sentence is style-related. Many writers and readers prefer an opening that will establish the broad context in a few sentences before the main aim of the chapter is reached. A thesis statement can be as powerful at the end of an opening paragraph as it is at the beginning.

c) Quotations

Fifty years ago, the norm for erudite academic writing was often to begin a text with a Latin quotation. This was considered good practice in terms of stylishness and elegance at least in the arts and humanities. Nowadays, quotations tend to be selected for their relevance as much as for the impact that they will make on the reader.

Quotations can make a chapter introduction seem distinctive without the need for any excessive digression. If the quotation is clearly *separated from the rest of the text*, it can, in any case, be safely ignored whenever it is considered to be too great a distraction. However, when unsuitable quotations are *built into the opening lines of a text*, this can sometimes present a challenge to the reader. Consider the following extracts:

Box 6.5. Alternative introductions to a text

1. *Within the mosaic of states, nations and societies of Eastern Europe, language is a powerful index of nationality. The essence or soul of nationality, said Joshua Fishman in his study of Language and Nationalism in 1972, 'is not only reflected and protected by the mother tongue, but in a sense the mother tongue is itself ... the soul made manifest'. So, too, Dr Johnson who told Boswell that he was always sorry when any language is lost 'for languages are the pedigree of nations'.*
2. *In 1996 I was approached by a complete stranger while talking with a group of friends in the Slovak town of Banska Bystrica. His words of greeting, 'na Slovensku po slovensky!' translate as 'in Slovakia you should speak Slovak'.*

About fifteen years ago, I was asked to contribute a chapter for a book entitled 'Democracy and Cultural Diversity'. My chapter would focus on Slovakia, where I had lived for several years and carried out some research on language legislation. At the time, there was a nationalist government in Slovakia which had decided to instigate new language laws to ensure the supremacy of the Slovak language over Czech, Hungarian and English. One example is that according to the new laws, all foreign television programmes had to be dubbed in Slovak even if they were in Czech (a very similar language). I began to write my chapter under the title 'Slovakia: Language and National Unity'.

The extracts above represent two possible introductions to my chapter. I wanted to use the second extract to provide what I considered to be a powerful illustrative example of one of my major themes. At the time, there was a good deal of linguistic discrimination prevalent in the country, and this was exemplified by an unusual incident in which I was directly involved: When I was walking along a road with a friend, we were admonished by a man who ordered us to stop speaking English. The outrage of this citizen had stayed in my mind.

However, my editor had other ideas. Although he found the chapter interesting, he considered that the introductory section lacked resonance and style, sounding too anecdotal. He re-wrote my introduction, moving a quotation from an academic writer (Joshua Fishman) from another part of my text to the first paragraph. He then added a well-known quotation from the author and lexicographer Dr Johnson describing language as 'the pedigree of nations'. The rest of my text was left unchanged.

When I first read the opening words of this chapter, I had difficulty recognizing it as a piece of text that I had written. I protested, arguing that readers would not welcome a quotation from Dr Johnson that distracted from the text, added little to it and made it look derivative. However, the editor's word was final. To me, this illustrates the strength of feeling that readers may harbour with respect to the style of introductory sections. This editor considered that a well-written chapter should always start in a 'stylish' way. A compromise was finally reached, and I was allowed to keep my illustrative example if it were included in the second paragraph. However, the compromise included the condition that I should change the style once again, using 'the writer' rather than first-person 'I' to refer to myself.

This story demonstrates how academic readers who are also accustomed to communicating in writing may have very clear expectations of chapter opening sections. My editor had previously supervised large numbers of PhD students and would have advised them accordingly. It is clearly important to find out the expectations of your readers. If you shock, disappoint or distract them, miscommunication may result. If you are sometimes forced to alter your style to accommodate them, this may have to happen despite your reservations.

d) Illustrative narratives or anecdotes

My chosen approach of starting with an illustrative story can also present problems. When you tell a story, readers are unlikely to know where it is leading. If the story is succinct and illustrates its point clearly, your readers will be able to appreciate it and understand its purpose. If, however, you begin a chapter with a long narrative, readers may quickly become disoriented. In this case, I considered that my story was not only short enough but also original and powerful: it reflected an incident that had not been reported anywhere else and that had shocked me. Perhaps I wanted to include it to shock my readers in turn, but I considered that my story was not just a stylistic device but a central part of my chapter.

Identifying and highlighting chapter themes

After the opening sentences of a chapter, the following need to be the main considerations for an academic writer planning an introductory section:

- *establishing the scope and aims of the chapter* – what will be included and excluded, which issues will be considered in depth and which will be deferred
- *outlining the chapter structure* – while it could be argued that the table of contents can fulfil this role, your readers will appreciate some guidance built into the text indicating the directions that the chapter will follow
- *establishing your own position or 'angle'* – of particular importance in literature review chapters where the points of view of different writers will be discussed

Some writers who have no difficulty with the first two of these elements can find that the third is more problematic. The extract below, which begins an individual research paper included in a PhD thesis, includes a strong positional statement which is clear to the reader.

Box 6.6. A positional statement

Understanding disarmament, demobilization and reincorporation processes. Incentives and armed conflict contexts.

I have two scenarios for developing my research on incentives for engaging in a DDR process. The first one is based on the rebel organization and the second one is former combatants. This paper seeks to analyze the group incentives for making or engaging DDR. Therefore, I want to

→

> answer the following questions: why have some countries that have had peace processes decided to implement DDR programs? What is the relationship between conflict types, kinds of DDR and their outcomes? What can we learn from past experiences of DDR about the set of incentives faced by negotiators either from the government side and/or the rebel forces?
>
> My hypothesis here is that if the armed groups have strong economic incentives for fighting, they should be less likely to start a "real" DDR process, taking into account that their armed structures might become an army reserve keeping the established coordination networks which can be easily reactivated.

This type of approach will work for some projects but not others. You may prefer or be required to establish your standpoint in a less direct manner: It is also possible that your readers will share this preference. Although there are no straightforward 'one-size-fits-all' prescriptions for success, it is worth seeking out this type of example in your own disciplinary area. Explicitly stating your position so that readers will understand your underlying thinking will contribute significantly to the clarity of your text. This theme will be further developed in Chapter 8.

Concluding sections

Thody (2006: 161) presents some sensible 'design criteria' for chapter endings, which can be summarized as follows:

- Try to make the major findings or arguments within the chapter memorable.
- Include an overview of what has been said in the chapter, and make sure that readers have been provided with any information that they will need in order to understand chapter content.

Surprisingly, very few other authors choose to focus on this area of writing. To address the gap, it is hoped that the points listed below will provide a degree of practical support. Concluding sections of individual thesis chapters may do any of the following:

1. *Summarize key arguments that have been presented.*
   It can be argued that for some complex chapters in particular, there is merit in repeating key arguments. Pulling all of the different strands of

the chapter together may help the reader to absorb and remember the important points that you have made. For other chapters, this type of repetition may be unnecessary and unwanted.

2. *Examine the implications of arguments presented in a chapter.*

 As is the case in the conclusion chapter of your thesis, an important question to ask is, 'What does all of this mean?' The only problem is that at the chapter level you may not be able to do justice to this question without producing an excessively long piece of text.

3. *Provide a 'high-impact ending' to the chapter.*

 There are dangers in high-impact endings, as there are for high-impact beginnings. However, if you can make readers remember your words (see Thody's criteria above), the risk may be worth taking from time to time.

4. *Look forward to the next chapter, providing clear links.*

 A convention within TV drama series is that a preview of the next episode will raise interest and motivate viewers to tune in. Whether this same technique can work in an academic thesis is uncertain. Links between chapters are necessary, but may be more appropriately placed at the beginning of the following chapter. You will also need to avoid generating wrong expectations in this way: it is quite easy to promise content that you then forget to deliver.

Task 6.1: Evaluating a second-draft table of contents

Earlier in this chapter, the first draft of a table of contents was presented for discussion. The following year, the same writer submitted an updated version. This is reproduced below.

What changes have been made?
Which of the changes appear to have improved the structural framework?
Are there any problem areas that remain?

Buddhist minorities in India: a Human Rights perspective and its legal implications

Chapter 1: Introduction

1.1. Main aims of this thesis
1.2. Wider context and analytical framework
1.3. The structure and methodological underpinnings

Chapter 2: Historical Background

2.1. Historicity of India
2.2. The terms 'Hindu' and 'Hinduism'

→

2.3. Pre-eminence of Buddhism prior to the advent of Muslims in India
2.4. When, why and how Buddhism disappeared in India
2.5. Co-option of Buddhism into Brahmanism
2.6. Rediscovery of Buddhism by the British
2.7. Concerns of minorities during the British Raj
2.8. Buddhism and Buddhist laws in South Asia
2.9. Revival of Buddhism in India
2.10. Buddhist minorities in India

Chapter 3: Constitutional and Legislative Issues

3.1. Development of Constitutional Law in India vis-à-vis the minorities
3.2. Issues of minorities and the Constituent Assembly Debates
3.3. Article 25 of the Constitution of India
3.4. Reflection of Article 25 in other legislative instruments
3.5. Case law on the term 'Hindu' and on article 25 of the Constitution of India
3.6. The Hindu code and its 'Hindu' hegemony
3.7. Debates regarding the 'Application of Acts' of Hindu Code
3.8. Access to justice vis-à-vis the present Personal Laws of India
3.9. Issues stretching outside the ambit of s.7 of HMA, 1955
3.10. Case law on the issues of Buddhist minorities
3.11. Juristic writings
3.12. Overlapping vagueness between 'reconstruction' and 'deconstruction'
3.13. Legal pluralism and informality

Chapter 4: Human Rights Perspective

4.1. Definition of 'minorities' and minority rights discourse
4.2. Right against discrimination
4.3. Vulnerability during transition
4.4. Executive actions
4.5. Issue of reservations
4.6. Right to profess and practise one's own religion
4.7. Concoction and camouflaging of the religious sites

Chapter 5: Case Study – the Bodhgaya Temple

5.1. Introduction
5.2. History and importance of the Bodhgaya Temple
5.3. The Bodhgaya Temple Management Act 1949
5.4. Violation of articles 25 and 26 of the Constitution of India
5.5. Struggle for its emancipation

Chapter 6: Conclusion

6.1 Prospects and implications
6.2 Appropriateness of laws

1. Produce a <u>draft table of contents and abstract</u> for your research project. Use this table of contents as a structural framework that will help you plan your writing. Revise and complete this document as your research progresses.
2. Use your table of contents as a <u>'mediation document'</u> in discussions with your supervisor that will feed into the planning of chapter writing. Keep a record of alterations in your table of contents and abstract. It may be useful to compare different versions to identify changes in your thinking.
3. Consider the types of chapters that will need to be included in the final version of your thesis and place them within an <u>organizational hierarchy</u>.
4. Decide on and prepare to justify the number of chapters that you are likely to need in relation to reader expectations and the needs of your project. When dividing chapters into sections, <u>avoid over-organization and under-organization</u>. Observe disciplinary conventions for headings and the numbering of sections.
5. Pay attention to <u>chapter sequencing</u> so that the order matches the development of argumentation within the thesis.
6. Pay attention to the <u>wording of chapter headings and subheadings</u>: these will act as important signposts for readers and should be precise, accurate, consistent in their use of terminology and meaningful.
7. Carefully plan <u>chapter introductions and conclusions</u> to fit into your framework. These will provide readers with a clear map to guide them through each chapter and to help them understand its role within the thesis.

7 Establishing Productive Writing Routines

This chapter

- *considers the role of productive routines in first draft thesis writing*
- *examines how the setting of specific tasks or goals can contribute to a writing routine*
- *discusses different ways in which writers engage with their texts*
- *considers the importance of feedback on writing and the role of the supervisor*
- *advises on how to respond to written and oral feedback*

A structural framework for a PhD thesis such as a table of contents is only, as Umberto Eco (2015) points out, 'a working hypothesis'. An additional element is necessary if your plan is to be of practical value – the allocation of time. One of the reasons for the growing popularity of 'New Route' PhDs is, I would argue, because they help PhD researchers allocate time more effectively due to their structured nature. In the more traditional model of PhD research, it is mostly the responsibility of the researcher to manage time. Nowhere is this more difficult than in the planning of writing.

▶ Goals, schedules and routines

The time that you have available for writing needs to be carefully broken down so that writing tasks can be allocated to time slots. A first step might be to try the following simple quiz.

Box 7.1. Goals, schedules and routines quiz for writing

1. When are you at your most productive: 8 a.m., 3 p.m., 9 p.m., 2 a.m.? Or does it vary?
2. Which days of the week will be dedicated to the PhD?
3. How many months of the year will be mainly dedicated to PhD work and which will not?
4. How much writing would you expect to produce in a day that is dedicated to writing – 250, 500, 1000 words?
5. Where do you prefer to read/write?
6. How do you prefer to write?

There are different aspects of setting goals, and there are different aspects of planning, some of which appear to receive more attention than others. Here is an example of a question which deserves your full attention: When are you *most productive*? Alternatively, when are you *least productive*?

My own answers to these questions would be early in the morning (most productive) and late at night (least productive). However, this has not always been the case: I can remember writing essays late into the night when I was in my early 20s. It seems that different people have different body rhythms which can change over a period of time. According to Morgan (2013), the teenage brain typically requires nine hours of sleep, but the teenage body clock tends to switch off only late at night. There are obvious consequences the next morning with parents having to force teenage children to get up for school. An equivalent would perhaps be an adult forced to wake up in the middle of the night on a regular basis. It also seems that some schools in the UK have now realized that timetables created by adults may not enable teenage students to be at their most productive and are beginning to conduct a series of experiments with starting times. (See Appendix 1 for further details.) A later starting-time will allow the teenage brain to reach its peak activity early in the afternoon.

When writing a long and complex academic text, it is essential that you should know when you are most productive and use this knowledge to your advantage. This means establishing suitable writing routines. If you are the type of person who can write in the morning, plan your time accordingly. However, it is almost certain that problems will arise as soon as your morning writing routine enters into conflict with other routines and the routines of those around you. You will need to be prepared for this situation. A typical example would be when 'peak writing times' clash with times when you need to be working somewhere else, perhaps in the office or teaching a scheduled class.

The biographies of famous writers clearly demonstrate the importance of writing routines. Novelist Graham Greene would get up at 6am every morning, go to his desk and start writing. He would then have breakfast at about 9am. This was a routine that never varied. In reaction to this, you may argue that he was a professional writer and his situation was therefore different, to which I would respond that at certain stages of your PhD and during your subsequent academic career, writing will be your main occupation. You will have stopped collecting your data, you will have done most of your reading and you will be writing full-time. It is a daunting prospect for many researchers.

To seek inspiration for establishing productive writing routines, there is a useful website, http://dailyroutines.typepad.com/, which documents the routines of public figures in many areas of professional activity, including writing. There are also classifications according to preferences. It seems that some people (including, for example, novelist Will Self) can be classified as 'early risers', whereas others might be labelled 'night owls'. Franz Kafka was a good example of the latter, beginning his writing regularly at 11 p.m. and continuing even until 6 a.m. on occasions, depending on his energy and resilience levels. Once the writing session had been completed, he would set off for his daytime job as chief clerk at an insurance company.

▶ When will you write? How will you allocate time?

Questions 2 and 3 in my 'Goals, Schedules and Routines Quiz' will help to further break down a writing routine. In terms of PhD thesis writing, this will normally be by means of:

1. monthly plans
2. daily schedules

The monthly plan is the preferred option for many writers. Here is a greatly adapted version of an example produced by a student in his third year of PhD study who went to consult his supervisor after a year's absence, collecting research data. At this point his supervisor suggested that he should perhaps make a six-month plan and then begin writing.

Box 7.2. A sample monthly plan for writing

<u>January</u>
- Meet with supervisor to agree on writing plan
- Develop detailed plan with timeframes

→

- Transcribe data transcripts, arrange data reporting formats (5 days)
- Flesh out chapter outlines

February

- Write/submit 1st draft of Chapter 1 (10 days)
- Transcribe transcripts, arrange data (5 days)
- Flesh out chapter outlines (ongoing)

March

- Write/submit 1st draft of Chapter 2 (10 days)
- Transcribe transcripts, arrange data (5 days)
- Review and take notes, new theoretical literature (3 days)
- Flesh out chapter outlines (ongoing)

April

- Write/submit 1st draft of Chapter 3 (10 days)
- Begin 1st draft of Chapter 4 (5 days)
- Flesh out chapter outlines (ongoing)
- Review chapter-by-chapter feedback from supervisor (3 days)

May

- Complete/submit 1st draft of Chapter 4 (5 days)
- Write/submit 1st draft of Chapter 5 (15 days)
- Review chapter-by-chapter feedback from supervisor (3 days)

June

- Write/submit 1st draft of Chapter 6 (10 days)
- Holiday break (7 days)
- Write/submit 1st draft of the Introduction (5 days)

I met the same student several months later and asked him about his writing and whether his plan had been successful. Predictably, it had proved to be unrealistic for a number of reasons. From our discussions, however, I began to realize that such plans have the following advantages:

1. Having a plan is always better than having no plan. A monthly plan is a statement of intent and an attempt to rationalize a complex process.
2. A written plan serves as a point of reference and as a useful mediation document with supervisors and other potential readers.
3. A written plan can help draw a distinction between different types of writing. In this case 'transcribing', 'fleshing out chapter outlines', 'writing chapters' and 'reviewing feedback' are all included.

These seem to be the disadvantages of this particular plan:

- an unrealistic and over-optimistic time allocation
- a linear time allocation, indicating that writing is seen only as the end product of thinking rather than a means of clarifying thinking. Chapter 1 in February is followed by Chapter 2 in March and Chapter 3 in April. This is unlikely to relate to reality
- no consideration of other aspects of life, apart from a one-week break from writing in June. How does this plan match other commitments? When planning months of activity, it is important to provide some flexibility and not to over-plan

The final point shows the real deficiency of monthly plans. They provide an overview of possible time allocation but rarely recognize the fact that in some months, you will be able to make substantial progress with your writing while in others there will be other commitments in daily life to prevent you from doing so. This is why some kind of varying weekly schedule is also essential.

How does such a schedule work? The answer is that it may need to be planned on the basis of a 'deficit model', eliminating times that will not be available for writing or reading and then carefully organizing the hours that remain. You will also need to consider when you are most and least productive. Routines might also be organized around more practical considerations: for example, if you have young children, you may only have the option of writing at night when they are asleep. A sample writing schedule is provided below (based on Zerubavel 1999: 26). Note that:

- All *dark shaded areas are unavailable for writing*. In some cases, specific appointments have been entered in these slots. Others are kept free for sleeping, family time, travelling or leisure activities. Sunday and Monday have been designated as free days.
- All *light shaded areas have been allocated as regular writing/reading* times: from these, it is evident that the person concerned prefers a morning writing routine.
- *White squares are available for scheduling more writing,* if needed.

While this approach can provide the basis for a regular weekly schedule, the actual writing activities (and therefore the writing schedule) will vary from week to week. Breaking down writing into separate activities can seem difficult but is an essential step in developing a productive routine.

Table 7.1 Sample weekly writing schedule

	Monday	Tuesday	Wednesday	Thursday	Friday	Saturday	Sunday
6.00							
7.00			Chapter 3: 1st draft	Chapter 3: 1st draft	Data report		
8.00			Chapter 3: 1st draft	Chapter 3: 1st draft	Data report		
9.00			Chapter 3: 1st draft			Shopping	
10.00		Teaching	Reading	Chapter 2 finish	Re-reading	Shopping	
11.00		Teaching	Reading	Chapter 2	Re-reading	Shopping	
12.00			Reading				
13.00			Reading		Teaching		
14.00		Staff Meeting			Teaching		
15.00				Supervisor Meeting			
16.00				Supervisor Meeting			
17.00							
18.00							
19.00			Eating out with family				
20.00			Eating out with family				
21.00			Eating out with family				
22.00			Eating out with family				
23.00							
0.00							

Zerubavel (1999) provides useful advice in this area from his own experiences of PhD thesis writing. He realized that there were certain times when he expected to be most productive and that it would be useful to allocate the most complex forms of writing to these periods. This might include any first draft chapter writing tasks, but in particular the production of pieces of text in which key concepts or theoretical frameworks were being explored, where source references were being analysed or where conclusions were being drawn based on an analysis of data. He labelled such tasks 'Type A writing'. Simpler tasks, including data transcribing, preparing a bibliography or producing a descriptive narrative, were labelled 'Type B writing'. His recommendation is that writers should try to allocate the most difficult Type A tasks for times when they know that they will be productive. If writers feel tired for some reason, there is always the option of switching to Type B tasks rather than stopping writing altogether.

This is practical advice that can make a real difference in the effective management of your time and also in maintaining your motivation to write. It is essential that 'quality time' is allocated for the most difficult and complex writing tasks. However, for this type of routine to work effectively, you will also need the cooperation of others, especially those who may believe that being a full-time PhD researcher allows you total flexibility in your daily life. Allocate your chosen hours for both writing (Type A and B) and reading activities – and then let other people know. Put your schedule in a prominent place at home or at work. When friends or family ask you to make yourself available at an inconvenient time, point out politely that this would shorten your scheduled writing time. Although first reactions may not always be positive, other people will gradually realize that you need to schedule writing time in the same way as teaching time or any other important activity. It is certainly worth making the effort to impose some order on your writing in this way.

Alternative approaches to time management are readily available, usually in the form of self-contained workshops. I attended one some years ago which left many people feeling somewhat depressed. The workshop leader asked all the participants to work out exactly how many months, weeks and hours they had left to complete their thesis and then divide their time according to the number of tasks requiring completion. This type of approach seems to assume that you can force yourself to meet a deadline just because it is there, accompanied by an apparent assumption that every hour is of equal value. Deadlines can help you remain focused on the tasks ahead, but they will only be of value if they are realistic. If you feel you are being given unreasonable targets by supervisors and others, you will need to query them. Living in a target-driven society can mean that sometimes you can aim too high. Both monthly plans and preferred routines will need to build in sufficient flexibility to allow you to readjust.

▶ Setting goals and targets

The fourth question in my 'goals, schedules and routines' quiz concerns the setting of manageable writing targets. How many words or pages should you aim for in a day? Would 500 words a day be a reasonable target? Here are the views of two PhD researchers:

> *I received the advice that if you write 500 words most days, you can have the whole thesis written within one year.* (1st-year PhD student, humanities)
> *I just write 250 words a day in order to put some ideas down.* (1st-year PhD student, law)

Using a quantitative approach may seem impractical if there is no consideration of the nature of the writing task. Making the calculation that writing 500 words per day will lead to early completion may also have failed to take into account that many texts will need to be rewritten three or four times. Is this sort of target setting therefore a waste of time?

I would argue that some kind of quantitative target is useful as a rough means of time allocation in the absence of a more effective system. Professional writers often build such targets into their regular routines, providing them with a useful reference point. A travel writer making the transition to academic writing reflects on her own target setting as follows:

> *I have research days and writing days and thinking days. So for a writing day, I will set a target of 1,000 words. I try to get all my ducks in a row, having done most of the reading and the thinking. Then I try and focus on getting down everything on paper for a first draft of 1,000 words. It is good to have a solid chunk of text to work with, even if I have to go back and re-edit.*

▶ Where and how will you write?

The final questions in the quiz refer to two different aspects of writing routines that are often taken for granted by research writers.

Where will you write?
When you talk to or read about professional writers, it is surprising how many of them have a favourite place in which to write. The room, the special desk, even the objects on the desk arranged in a certain way and the correct cup of coffee can all put them in the mood for writing. Their routine revolves not just around writing times but also around writing locations, which also

help them take control of their writing. Some examples of locations and accompanying rituals can be found at http://dailyroutines.typepad.com and include the following:

- *Stephen King* starts work from 8:00 to 8:30. He takes a vitamin pill, switches on favourite music, always sits in the same seat and has papers all arranged in the same places.
- *Vladimir Nabukov* used to wake between 6:00 and 7:00 every morning. He wrote until exactly 10:30, standing at a lectern which faced a bright corner of the room. This ritual appears to have motivated him to write because it reminded him of his days as a lecturer speaking to an enthusiastic audience of young people.

There is also one example of a strong view about where <u>not</u> to write:

- *Orhan Pamuk* believes that the place where you sleep or the place that you share with your partner should be separate from the place where you write.

Some writers, however, prefer to vary the places where they write. After carefully studying my cat, who prefers to spend two weeks in one place (on the window sill) and then two weeks somewhere else (on a chair), I decided to try this approach in my writing and found it to be quite productive. In my case, I spent two weeks writing in the library, followed by two weeks at home in a particular room. The results were positive, so it seems that there is also an argument to be put forward for changing location if this helps with self-motivation.

How will you write?

A related question concerns how you will write. To be more precise, 'How will you physically engage in the act of writing?'. This aspect of writing is rarely considered, even though advances in technology have resulted in radical changes in behaviour. Here are some specific questions to consider:

- Do you prefer to write ideas down directly on a PC screen as they occur to you?
- Do you make rough notes on paper and then type them up?
- Do you write a first draft on paper and then carefully type it out?
- Do you prepare a typed skeleton structure with headings and subheadings and then begin to fill in the gaps?
- Do you ever use audio recordings of yourself thinking aloud as input for writing?

- Do you make use of Post-its (handwritten) or electronic Stickies (typed) to provide you with writing input?
- Do you make use of mind maps?
- Do you ever use speech recognition software to note down your stream-of-consciousness thoughts?
- Do you use combinations of these techniques? Which ones?
- Do you vary techniques according to the writing task?

A survey of several groups of PhD research writers provided an interesting range of responses to these questions:

I use most of the techniques – and also notecards. I can't just sit down and start typing.

Most respondents shared these views, experiencing difficulties in transferring ideas in their head directly onto a screen as part of first draft writing. In cases where this happened, the type of writing was described as 'exploratory' or 'a prelude to something else', and there was an expectation that it would be extensively revised later. Producing a finished text by committing ideas directly to a screen was not considered a realistic option. However, one person disagreed: '*I write stream-of-conscious right onto the screen and then edit. I can't write on paper. Now if I try to think creatively on paper, I can't do it. I am also too slow on paper – I type faster than I can write.*'

One respondent made regular use of mind maps as an input to writing because: 'they can help me focus on the central theme of the chapter, and it's surprising how often this can change'. If you are trying to unpack key concepts or explain complex theories, mind maps can be useful. There is also the possibility that your mind map may be of sufficiently good quality to include as part of your written text.

Audio-recorded notes can also provide useful input for first draft writing, especially in the case of chapters in which managing all of the content and committing it to paper or screen seem problematic. A partial transcription of the recording might feed directly into a first draft chapter section. The advantage of audio-recorded notes is that they can include detailed information that you might otherwise have forgotten. It is not always possible to rush to the computer to write down ideas, but it is relatively easy to switch on a phone and record your voice. Otherwise, there is always the danger that a brilliant idea can be lost if you are prevented from writing it down in time.

Finally, my own writing routine changed forever when I bought an extra monitor for my computer. Like many other writers, I now find it hard to imagine how I could have produced anything of value without making use of two monitors. On monitor 1, you can work on your finished document while you compare, copy or paste text fragments from monitor 2. This simple change can transform the ease of writing and (arguably) encourages more creativity as well as greater productivity. Staring at one screen encourages linear thinking. Looking across from one screen to another can help you compare different texts, move pieces of text around, organize ideas more effectively and (on occasions) engage in some lateral thinking.

▶ **Feedback on writing**

In the sample monthly plan reported earlier, it was interesting to note that 'reviewing supervisor feedback' had been entered as a scheduled activity. This type of approach should be encouraged because requesting, analysing and responding to feedback is an important part of any productive writing routine. The first step is to build regular *self-monitoring* into the writing process. What have you written so far? What problem areas have you encountered in writing and in reading? What kind of written and oral feedback have you received? How does this compare to your own evaluation?

When I consulted a group of 1st-year PhD researchers concerning their self-monitoring of problem areas in reading and writing, some interesting results emerged. The problems that they identified are, I believe, fairly typical and have been summarized below:

Box 7.3. Problem areas related to reading

1. Not being able to skim and scan. Having to read things twice and keep going back so that ideas can be transferred to note cards in preparation for writing.
2. Because information is disseminated across a number of different disciplines, texts have to be read very intensively so as not to miss ideas. As sometimes section labels are not helpful, it is difficult to skip any of the sections. The result is that everything has to be read slowly and carefully.
3. Taking notes at this level sounds easy but it is not just a question of summarizing a few ideas at a basic level. When responding to a text, it is hard to know first of all what to analyse and then how to analyse it.
4. Going off at a tangent as a result of reading. It is possible to become so interested in what we read that we do not realize that this is happening.
5. Some non-academic source materials and materials in other languages are inaccessible.

Box 7.4. Problem areas related to writing

1. Compulsive rewriting of what has been written because thinking can change – this way it is possible to end up writing four drafts or more, which can also change.
2. Managing the process of drafting and redrafting can be extremely difficult – if you redraft too many times before putting everything down on paper in a coherent fashion, you may forget your starting point.
3. Time management.
4. Conflicting pieces of text when you find that you are contradicting yourself in different sections of your work.
5. Distancing yourself from your writing.

To identify other problem areas in writing and the process of turning reading into writing, the next stage is to consider *peer feedback* and to compare it with your own impressions. Sometimes, what writers really need is to gain a rough sense of whether the gist of a text and its main arguments can be clearly understood, especially in cases where self-monitoring leads to doubts or uncertainty in this respect. The kind of questions that you can put to your readers (even those from other disciplines) could be as follows:

- How much of this text did you understand? (50 per cent? 75 per cent? 100 per cent?)
- Are the aims of the text clear?
- Does the text seem to be clearly structured?
- What is the main argument? Is it clearly articulated?
- How effectively are supporting arguments developed?
- Are the arguments backed by convincing evidence?
- Are the key concepts fully explored and explained?
- Do you have any comments on the introduction or conclusion sections?
- Do you have any comments on language or style?

For many years, I have run courses in which PhD research writers are encouraged to submit samples of their work in order to receive this kind of feedback from their peers. The written texts are accompanied by an oral presentation by the authors, explaining the context and aims of their research and locating the sample text that has been circulated within their PhD thesis. Most writers find this to be a useful and encouraging experience. They appreciate knowing that their text can be understood, however technically specialized the content might be. The knowledge that the main arguments are being clearly communicated to interested readers is also reassuring.

The next type of feedback to be considered is that which is provided by *PhD supervisors*. In general, your supervisor can be expected to provide three different kinds of feedback:

1. overall written feedback at the end of a text
2. detailed written feedback in the form of text annotations
3. oral feedback delivered in tutorials

PhD supervisors have different supportive roles, according to Rugg and Petre (2004: 34). These authors categorize supervisory activities in the following terms:

- specific technical support
- broader intellectual support
- administrative support
- management
- personal support

It seems that the first two areas of support include help with critical thinking relating to the content of research, finding source materials, networking with other researchers and providing guidance on structuring the thesis. The other three are self-explanatory. There is no explicit mention of any support for writing, apart from some giving some hints on finding a suitable structure. This is a significant omission from the detailed list of activities that these authors (and others) provide.

The exception is Wisker (2005), who dedicates an entire chapter of her *Good Supervisor* handbook to 'encouraging good writing' and argues that the supervisor has an important role in this respect. Her advice for supervisors to pass on to their PhD student writers can be summarized very briefly:

- Get ideas down on paper at an early stage to help the process of critical thinking.
- Learn the disciplinary conventions for writing and 'disciplinary discourse'.
- Clarify expectations of the structure of the thesis.
- Keep good notes.
- Record ideas in a research journal, and write reflectively.
- Practise two types of writing – 'conceptual' and 'critically engaged'.
- Discuss any blocks to writing with sympathetic listeners.

These are certainly appropriate examples of ways in which your PhD supervisor could help you greatly with your written text. The problem is that many individual supervisors fail to realize that this is an important role that they can play, while others are concerned that they will become distracted from their main role of supplying technical support relating to the content and methodology of your research project. In many cases it will be up to you, the writer, to elicit this type of help from one of your intended readers. The role that all supervisors do recognize is that of *feedback provider*. Most will expect to provide you with all three types of feedback mentioned at the beginning of this section, which we will now consider in greater detail.

You can reasonably expect that any text that you submit to a supervisor will be returned to you annotated with specific feedback comments. Usually, these will be accompanied by some overall impressionistic comments at the end. The summative comments will need to be supported by evidence in the text itself. 'Lacks analysis' is not a particularly useful comment unless there is an indication of the type of analysis that is lacking and the specific points in the text where further analysis appears to be required. As the recipient, you have to understand all of the feedback. If it is unclear, it will need to be queried at the earliest opportunity. Thinking of such feedback *not as an end product but as part of an ongoing dialogue* makes it natural to make this request.

You will need feedback on the content of your text (which is what supervisors expect to provide), but feedback on the quality of your writing is also necessary. Supervisors are generally highly skilled and experienced academic writers. Many tend to write intuitively without really being aware of their skill levels: most also appear to enjoy writing. In the final chapter of this handbook, I will report on a piece of research in which academics talk about the importance of writing throughout an academic career.

One important aspect of any productive routine for PhD research writing is how you respond to the feedback that you receive, whether written or oral. Feedback delivered orally as part of a tutorial has the immediate advantage that it can be queried on the spot. For feedback discussion to be effective there are certain conditions that will need to be fulfilled:

- Both you and your supervisor will need to *listen carefully* to each other and allow each other to explain any differences in views.
- You will need *to record the discussion*. An audio recording often works best, but it is always a good idea to agree to this in advance. Written notes can also be effective.
- If you do not understand the feedback received, *you must try to clarify*. Do not give up after a first attempt. Do not give the impression that you have

understood if this is not the case. It is better to lose face by admitting ignorance, rather than allowing an opportunity for clarification to slip by. In many cases, the problem will be due to your supervisor's inability to communicate rather than your inability to understand.

- You *do not need to respond to criticisms of your written work immediately.* Avoid putting yourself in situations where you feel the need to defend yourself at all costs. If you ask for time to think about the feedback and provide a measured response at a later date, this will normally be acceptable.
- There is *no obligation to accept your supervisor's criticisms.* Having thought through the feedback very carefully, if you feel that the criticism is unjustified, be prepared to argue your case during the next tutorial.

Finally, if you ask for feedback, be prepared to receive unexpected responses from time to time. I was once asked to comment on a written dissertation in which I noticed that the writing style was inconsistent. The writer began by using a simple, straightforward academic style in her first two chapters. Chapter 3, the methodology chapter, then adopted a completely different style before inexplicably changing back again. It was as if the writer had suddenly changed personality. The end result was a rather pompous-sounding, jargon-ridden piece of text (at least that is how it seemed to a non-specialist reader).

When I pointed this out, the writer became upset. She had thought to herself that she needed to adopt a really serious style for this particular section explaining the foundations of her research. She claimed that other writers in the field (psychology) would do exactly the same and that there was almost a requirement to adopt a more serious tone when considering the important question of research foundations. My point was that she had asked for my honest feedback and I had provided it. Her point was that my feedback was both unhelpful and demoralizing. Such situations can occur at any point during the research process. Our response to negative feedback should be to consider it carefully on its merits, decide on our response and then move on.

Action Points

1. Consider how the time that you have available for writing can be broken down so that writing tasks can be allocated. Prepare two key documents to help with this: a monthly plan and a weekly schedule.
2. Write a monthly plan as a mediation document for discussions with your supervisor and as a guide for the writing process. Be prepared to make changes as your research develops.

3. Maintain a <u>weekly schedule</u> for both reading and writing. Place this in a prominent place, consult it regularly and change it as required. Consider the times when you will be most productive and schedule the most demanding and complex writing accordingly.
4. Specify <u>quantitative writing targets</u> with your supervisor. Adjust, as required.
5. Pay attention to <u>where you write</u> and <u>how you write</u> so that effective writing routines may be developed and maintained.
6. Build <u>regular self-evaluation</u> into the writing process. Identify problem areas and discuss them with your peers as well as supervisors. Make sure that you fully understand feedback from others. Clarify whenever this is necessary. Think carefully before responding to negative feedback. A defensive attitude may prevent you from fully appreciating other points of view.

8 Writing Clearly, Concisely and Coherently

> *This chapter*
>
> * *identifies ways of achieving clarity and conciseness at sentence level*
> * *proposes some principles relating to coherence at paragraph and chapter levels*
> * *discusses ways of balancing the demands of academic style conventions against the need for clarity*

► Clarity and coherence

One of the requirements of every PhD thesis is that you produce a text containing ideas that are communicated to your readers in a clear and coherent way. At the same time, you are expected to write in a suitable academic style, determined partly by the discourse of your particular disciplinary area and partly by a perception of a more general academic style.

The problem faced by all thesis writers is that clarity, coherence and style can easily enter into conflict with each other, with style acting as an obstacle to clarity. If taken to excess, the result can be texts that consist of turgid, impenetrable prose or pompous rhetoric. A further complication is that certain texts might be rejected by some readers on these grounds, while other readers may be prepared to accept a loss of clarity in favour of adherence to stylistic conventions.

When PhD supervisors in the UK talk about clarity and style, they may refer you to an essay written by George Orwell in 1946 (*Politics and the English Language*), in which he identifies what he considers to be the 'mental vices' that affect the clarity and coherence of writing: 'dying metaphors' (used without understanding their meaning), 'verbal false limbs' (phrases with redundant elements), 'pretentious diction' and 'meaningless words'.

Orwell's suggested rules for clear writing come at the end of his essay and act as a warning against overuse of metaphors and imagery, excessively complex words, redundant words and sentences, technical expressions that have an everyday equivalent and the use of the passive rather than the active voice.

Rules such as these provide a simple prescription for all forms of writing and remain influential because of their creator's status as a writer and as a public figure. For academic writing, working within varying stylistic conventions and constraints, they might not provide the most useful or practical starting point: a more appropriate and more flexible set of guidelines will be required.

Clarity at sentence level

Let us begin by considering the nature of 'clear sentences'. Following the example of Williams (1995), this is probably best achieved by examining sample sentences that appear to lack clarity in some way. This may be experienced as partial or total incomprehensibility or as ambiguity of meaning. The language used may be considered unclear at word, phrase or sentence level. In some cases, the immediate context might help to clarify the meaning of the sentence, while in others it may not.

The following sentences are taken from an adapted version of an essay written by a postgraduate student under the heading 'The positive effects of correcting second language learner errors' and are presented in the exact sequence in which they appear in a single paragraph within the text. The three sentences have been numbered for convenience.

Box 8.1. Problems of clarity

(1) *If it is necessary to have a close scrutiny of error correction in terms of second language learning, the process and purpose of learning the target language should be put in the foreground, so that the motivation of error correction from teachers would be more acceptable and accountable for learners.* (2) *Bartram (1991) stated that language learners should go through a series of long-term learning processes within a natural environment in order to accumulate a great amount of language knowledge to attain a productive outcome.* (3) *During the periods of this process, the outcome produced might be a mirror of comprehension of language knowledge, but, more importantly, the feedback that teachers provide fosters the development of language learners.*

What do these sentences mean? How difficult is it to pinpoint the precise arguments that are being presented? The first sentence is certainly easier to understand if it is rewritten as follows:

> *Language teachers need to highlight the process and the purpose of learning certain target language items when focusing on error correction. This will help motivate learners to accept the correction of their errors.*

Why might this version be preferable? What changes have been applied to make it more accessible to the reader? It seems that the first version is more difficult for readers to understand because:

- the main action within the sentence, 'to put in the foreground' (more simply expressed as 'to highlight'), is relatively hard to identify
- the main subject of the sentence 'teachers' or 'language teachers' is also hard to identify and is located towards the end rather than at the beginning
- the use of the passive 'be put in the foreground' rather than the active 'put in the foreground' or 'highlight' is a further complication that makes it more difficult for the reader to understand the logic of the sentence

In taking these points into account, the rewritten version of the sentence *places the main subject and the main action in the most prominent position possible* – at the very beginning. Use of the passive is avoided as there is no apparently compelling reason to include it. Further problems of clarity in sentence 1 include the following:

- abstract nouns and adjectives such as 'motivation' or 'acceptable' are preferred to verbs ('motivate', 'accept')
- some of the language seems rather vague – what is meant, for instance, by expressions such as 'the process and the purpose' or 'accountable for learners'?

The first of these is a common phenomenon in academic texts. Some writers tend to bury important actions within abstract nouns, doing so intuitively rather than deliberately. Thus, 'the motivation of error correction' is preferred to 'motivating learners when correcting their errors'. Creating a string of resonant abstract nouns can make the style of the text appear more formal and therefore 'more academic'. However, if clarity is sacrificed in order to achieve this, there is a danger that the most important information will not be transmitted to the reader.

As far as vague language is concerned, an important task at the editing stage will be to weed out any sources of obscurity or ambiguity. In this case, what precisely is meant by 'if it is necessary to have a close scrutiny of error correction'? Could this be more clearly expressed by means of a verbal phrase such as 'carefully examine ways in which teachers correct errors'? Arguably, vague language is also a problem in sentences 2 and 3 with the use of expressions such as 'outcome' (where this is not specified) or 'long-term learning processes' (also unspecified).

How would we respond as a reader if we came across sentence 1 as part of a text? A natural reaction would be to move on in the hope that in the next sentence ideas will become clearer. This solution will usually work in the case of a rogue aberrant sentence. If, however, every sentence is written in a similar style, the coherence of the text will break down since text level coherence begins with clarity at sentence level. If a writer persists in writing in this style, it is likely that the reader will get lost, and there will be further consequences which are outlined in the final section of this chapter.

In the specific example given above, sentences 2 and 3 are not particularly helpful in explaining sentence 1. Sentence 3 also appears difficult to decipher, raising certain questions:

- What 'process' is being referred to?
- What is the 'outcome' that is the subject of this sentence? Is it the 'real subject' in terms of meaning or simply the grammatical subject?
- How might this outcome act as 'a mirror of comprehension of language knowledge'?

To eliminate such sentences from the academic texts that we produce, it is sometimes necessary to ask questions with this level of detail. Williams (1995) proposes two simple principles that will help in this respect, summarized below:

- Whoever/whatever has performed the most meaningful action should also be the grammatical subject of the sentence.
- The most meaningful action in the sentence should also (wherever possible) be the grammatical verb.

However, there is an immediate problem when academic conventions in some disciplines are considered. Williams' advice would entail using expressions such as 'I will argue ...', 'I will show ...', 'We may cite ...', using active rather than passive constructions in sentences and clearly establishing the identities of those who perform each action. Many academic disciplines, however, make consistent use of what is sometimes called 'the institutional passive'. Rather than 'I will demonstrate ...', 'it will be demonstrated that ...' is preferred. Although ideas may seem less clear as a result, here is a convention that you may be obliged to consider if your writing is to meet the expectations of your readers. For an interesting and more detailed examination of how and why academic disciplines can vary in this respect, see the research conducted by Harwood (2005).

Such examples demonstrate how clarity and style can be in opposition. How you deal with this conflict and achieve a suitable balance between them is an important aspect of your writing. Circumstances may dictate that in certain disciplines you will have less licence to be stylistically clear. In any area of inquiry, it is likely that you will have to observe certain conventions that will make clarity a little more difficult to achieve.

Coherence at paragraph level

Having briefly considered some issues of clarity at sentence level, the next step is to ask yourself how your clear sentences can be combined into paragraphs in such a way that the ideas contained in them develop in a coherent manner. Williams (1995: 48) once again provides initial guidance. He suggests three principles, the first two of which are closely related:

> *Put at the beginning of a sentence those ideas that you have already mentioned, referred to, or implied, or concepts that you can reasonably assume your reader is already familiar with, and will readily recognize.*
>
> *Put at the end of your sentence the newest, the most surprising, the most significant information: information that you want to stress – perhaps the information that you will expand on in your next sentence.*

These two principles describe a linear process, arguing that coherence in a text is more likely to be achieved if the beginning of each sentence is located in familiar territory. The flow of ideas can then be achieved by adding new information, which will become the starting point of the following sentence. The process might be summarized as *'something old, something new'*.

However, such principles alone are unlikely to guarantee a coherent text. It is possible, for example, that you may find yourself embarking on an endless journey, with each new piece of information causing you to set off in a slightly different direction. There is no indication of how you might build arguments in a logical fashion or avoid circularity. For the two principles to work effectively, they must become subject to an overriding principle of coherence, which operates at whole-text level:

> *A reader will feel that a paragraph is coherent if (s)he can read a sentence that specifically articulates its point.* (Williams 1995: 97)

Paragraphs can be considered the building blocks of all but the shortest texts. Each paragraph acts as a 'unit of meaning' which will add new information or fresh analysis to what has already been written. To achieve coherence both within and between paragraphs in the mind of the reader, sentences that make the main idea explicit can make a real difference. The reader will no longer need to wonder 'what is this piece of text about?' or 'what is this author trying to tell me?'. The answer to such questions will be prominently displayed. Similarly, at the beginning of a chapter or of a research paper, articulating the main point(s) can contribute significantly to the overall coherence of the text.

This does not necessarily mean a definitive statement of intent in the very first sentence of a paragraph or of a longer text. It does mean, however, that at an early stage you will need to clearly signal your intentions to the reader so that a sense of direction is established. Readers appreciate knowing where a text is heading and hold a reasonable expectation that they will not be kept in the dark. Writers, on the other hand, may enjoy creating a certain amount of suspense and may also fear spelling out their message too explicitly so as not to insult the reader. If you are finding it difficult to curb such tendencies, you may find it useful to repeat to yourself the words 'when in doubt, spell it out'.

How do the principles of clarity and coherence work when applied to academic writing? In terms of clarity at sentence level, a text that you produce can be carefully examined for potential problem areas. These might include examples of:

- unnecessarily long or complex sentences
- unnecessarily short disconnected sentences
- overuse of abstract nouns
- complex structures where grammar and meaning do not match
- repetition (unintentional and/or with no clear purpose)
- redundancy
- gratuitous jargon
- vagueness or ambiguity
- excessive imagery or obscurity

In terms of coherence at paragraph level, your text could also be carefully examined for potential problem areas. These might include examples of:

- the main point of the text or its underlying purpose not being clear
- the main point of the text being hidden (for example, in the middle of a very long paragraph)

- the main point of the text appearing very late, causing the reader to speculate on the direction of the arguments
- disconnection of ideas, where new arguments do not appear to follow logically from old ones
- circularity of argumentation, leading the reader back to point A rather than progressing smoothly to point B
- significant digressions which result in the reader losing sense of direction

A fuller version of these checklists can be found in Chapter 13. Such questions can serve an important function in helping you monitor the progress of your writing with respect to its clarity and coherence levels. There is, however, a danger in taking self-criticism too far. Although sentence-level changes can provide greater ease of accessibility for the reader, the result could be a rather dull, less personalized piece of writing. You might even believe that in some ways the power of your own voice has been reduced and your ability to express yourself in a preferred style diminished.

When considering issues relating to sentence-level clarity and expectations of style, a useful exercise is to read certain sentences aloud. In the sample text above, for example, does 'put in the foreground' resonate more than the simpler alternative 'highlight'? As we have seen, it is possible to re-edit a text by eliminating examples of unnecessary imagery, repetition and redundancy. But would the text sound the same, and would we hear the writer's voice as powerfully? These questions are worth further consideration before applying principles of clarity and coherence with total efficiency. The extent to which academic writers should be allowed some latitude in this respect will be the theme of the next chapter.

▶ The nature of coherence

Coherence and structure

At this point it is useful to provide a broader interpretation of the concept of coherence without reference to any guiding principles. In particular, structure and coherence need to be compared. To illustrate the difference between them, consider the following texts. The first is adapted from a text proposed by Enkvist (1990: 12); the second has been fabricated:

1. *The net bulged with the force of the shot. The referee blew his whistle and signalled. Offside. The goalkeeper sighed with relief. The crowd started to jeer. Soon the slow handclapping started again. ...*

2. *Soil is a serious problem in many countries. Besides, around 7 million hectares of fertile land are lost in the world each year. On the contrary, about 10 million hectares of forest are being lost. Therefore, the consequences are indeed serious. ...*

The interesting feature of the second text is that coherence actually appears to increase if some of the discourse markers such as 'on the contrary' are removed. This demonstrates that text markers that are intended to act as clear signposts to the reader may actually have the opposite effect. In the first text, where no overt signposts are included, the text is readily understandable and coherence can be recognized, provided that certain conditions are fulfilled. In the second text, the discourse markers are either redundant or misleading.

What is happening in the second text is that a structure has been superimposed by means of discourse markers: 'besides' ... 'on the contrary' ... 'therefore'. The structure of the text thus seems clear, but this is not enough to achieve coherence. In contrast, the first text appears to achieve coherence without any clear structure. In fact, there is an inner structure available to the reader, but it is not explicit: the reader's task is to make sense of this, while the writer's task is to create the conditions to enable this to happen. To achieve coherence, it is not enough to divide a text into sections by using discourse markers such as 'firstly', 'secondly', 'on the other hand' or 'moreover'.

In this respect I once had the difficult task of persuading a writer whose first language was Korean that 'eighthly' and 'ninthly' might not be suitable expressions to start a sentence within an academic text. His argument was that they highlighted his ideas and made them clearer. He was prepared to accept that this might contravene accepted style conventions and that it is inadvisable to write 'seventhly' or 'fifthly' under normal circumstances. However, the argument that this use of language also fails on the grounds of clarity – turning texts into lists of items – was met with more resistance.

Returning to the first of our two texts, there needs to be a recognition that it is coherent only under certain conditions. Some background knowledge of what is taking place is required: in this case schematic knowledge of football (or possibly hockey), its vocabulary, rules and conventions. If this is present, then the text has coherence and the sequence of events can be followed. Otherwise, many of the events will be unclear: why, for instance, did the goalkeeper 'sigh with relief'? And who is the goalkeeper?

This is what coherence is about – applying our knowledge to enable ideas to emerge from a text in a meaningful way. Colomb and Griffin (2004) provide a useful explanation of what an absence of coherence might entail:

It is hard to define coherence. We know it when we see it. And we know where it comes from. Coherent texts hang together. Their ideas are consistent.

They stick to the topic. They have many ideas that hold the others in line. They don't wander. They don't have rogue parts that confuse us with their irrelevancies.

While we may not be able to define 'coherence' clearly, there are certain characteristics that we recognize and that help us to make sense of a text. The same authors continue:

Coherence is a mundane, largely invisible background to our own experience, emerging whenever our minds package what we perceive, imagine, or understand neatly enough for us to manage it within the limits of our conscious capacities for attention and intention. So mundane is it, that we typically notice coherence only in its absence.

The argument that discourse markers can add to the coherence of a text is difficult to resist. Writers for whom English is a foreign language, such as my Korean student, have often been taught to use: 'on the one hand ... on the other hand ...' and other such phrases. These 'linking expressions' may be of some value as markers of coherence (as well as markers of structure) when used sparingly, but their use is in fact very subtle. If we attempt to add discourse markers to the first text, it becomes apparent that they are redundant. A new version of the same text with the additional phrases underlined might be:

First of all, the net bulged with the force of the shot. Shortly after this, the referee blew his whistle and signalled. Offside. The goalkeeper sighed with relief. Suddenly, the crowd started to jeer. Soon the slow handclapping started again ...

Note how this begins to change the meaning of the text in the mind of the reader. The original sequence of events appears to be: a goal was scored ... the referee disallowed it ... the goalkeeper felt relieved ... the crowd were unhappy ... their unhappiness spread. There are some ambiguities, but we can recognize a sort of sequence, and we do not even realize that we are doing so. However, there is also a sense that some of the actions may be simultaneous rather than consecutive. With the use of rather clumsy structural markers, a more rigorous sequence of events is apparently imposed in which actions follow each other in systematic fashion. This impression is reinforced by the use of 'first of all' to begin the opening sentence. Previously only 'soon' fulfilled this type of role.

To sum up, it seems that coherence is not necessarily achieved by the addition of structural labels. In the worst cases, these can actually confuse the reader, make the meaning unclear and the whole text less coherent.

Coherence across cultures

Up to this point, we have assumed a shared understanding of the principles that underlie clear and coherent writing. However, in anticipating the expectations of our readers, can we always be certain that this is the case? If achieving coherence is dependent on our own experience, might an understanding of coherence be very different in other languages and in other cultures? The question is worth considering if we claim to be writing for an international audience.

The prevailing academic culture in the UK (and arguably in the USA) appears to be one in which considerations of clarity and coherence override other aspects of writing. Hinds (1987) labels such cultures 'writer responsible' as opposed to 'reader responsible'. In the former, there is an obligation on the part of the writer to make things clear while the reader is perceived to have a lesser responsibility in this respect. However, in other languages and associated cultures, the opposite may be true. In German academic texts, according to Siepmann (2006: 142), it is expected that the reader will share the writer's subject knowledge. There is therefore no need to state explicitly why the content is significant or to highlight important arguments within a clearly defined hierarchy. In English academic texts, Siepmann argues that *topic sentences* 'tend to control paragraph structure', whereas in German the use of topic sentences is less frequent and there is no 'unified model of paragraph structure' expected by readers.

Meanwhile, Hatim (1997) cited in Connor (2002), claims that texts in Arabic may be heavy in what he terms *through-argumentation*, with arguments and evidence presented in support of an initial thesis leading to a conclusion. He argues that the logic of this type of typical text is different from 'Western argumentation' which he believes places a strong focus on refuting counterarguments.

Linguists such as Siepmann (in the case of German texts), Hinds (Japanese texts) or Hatim (Arabic texts) are the first to emphasize that cross-cultural comparisons of coherence in texts should not lead to the conclusion that the UK model is in any way logically superior. Instead, writers need to be aware that the expectations of their readers with respect to text coherence may be partly culturally determined and to be prepared for this eventuality. Here is a useful preparation task which may be of particular value in cases where:

- you will write your thesis in English even though it is not your first language
- you sense that perceptions of coherence may be different when comparing English and your own first language

---

Task 8.1: Comparing perceptions of coherence

Choose an academic text that has been translated from a language that is familiar to you and that you consider may present problems of coherence to the reader. A short research paper of three or four pages containing at least six paragraphs would be ideal. Now consider the following questions:

1. Is the main point or aim of the text clearly articulated?
2. In which part of the text does the main point appear?
3. To what extent do the following contribute to overall coherence?
   • headings and subheadings
   • signposting and structural markers in the text
   • paragraphing
   • topic sentences introducing paragraphs
   • the ending of the text
4. Which of these problem areas appear in the text?
   • disconnected arguments
   • circular arguments
   • significant digressions

As a final step, find the original version of the text or produce your own translation. Do the same problem areas appear? Does the text appear to be more coherent in its original version than in the translation?

▶ Coherence at chapter level

To conclude this chapter, I provide a summary of how coherence needs to be achieved and maintained in longer pieces of text. At the level of the thesis chapter, coherence can be achieved on a consistent basis by means of:

• main points and the writer's position being articulated at the beginning
• headings and subheadings acting as clear indicators of content
• signposting within the text
• conciseness within the text that cuts out repetition and redundancy
• adherence to the 'something old, something new' principle
• clear paragraphing, with one idea per paragraph
• paragraph topic sentences
• interim summaries to reinforce arguments

The consequences of not paying attention to these indicators of coherence can become increasingly serious:

1. The reader *becomes confused and loses the thread of the argument*. As this is a common experience when reading 'difficult' texts, the usual reaction

will be to try to work out why this has happened by referring to the immediate context of preceding and subsequent pieces of text.

2. The reader *begins to feel cheated and misled* by the writer if referring to the immediate context does not help. Frustration begins to grow.
3. The reader's *impatience increases* as a direct result of constant re-reading of sentences and paragraphs in order to understand them and to refer them to a meaningful context.
4. The reader loses the plot and *can no longer see where the text is leading*.
5. The reader *loses faith and gives up*. At this point the reader may still not necessarily blame the writer, though the net effect will be the same irrespective of who is perceived to be at fault.

Readers who are attempting to gain an understanding of a difficult text can go through all of these stages. If you see that your readers are showing such symptoms, then immediate action is required. The feedback that you receive from supervisors and other readers is crucial to achieving adequate levels of clarity and coherence even in a first draft. The way in which you interpret and understand their feedback is of equal importance.

Action Points

1. Ensure that <u>individual sentences within your text are clear</u> by checking that the main actions and the main subject are prominently highlighted.
2. Ensure that <u>paragraphs develop coherently</u> by following the 'something old, something new' principle.
3. Ensure that <u>longer pieces of text develop coherently</u> by articulating the main point at an early stage.
4. Once a first draft of a chapter has been produced, <u>check sentence clarity and paragraph coherence</u> carefully.
5. Be aware in both reading and writing that <u>perceptions of coherence may differ across cultures.</u> Reader expectations of coherence need to be considered.

9 Developing Academic Style

This chapter

- *highlights an ongoing debate about 'difficult texts' and considers how style contributes to difficulty either intentionally or unintentionally*
- *provides examples of 'difficult texts' and categorizes them*
- *considers the balance between conventions of style and the need for clarity, conciseness and coherence*

▶ Expectations of academic style

Academic conventions

Attention to academic style tends to be associated with the editing rather than the first draft writing stage, but it is never too early to develop a finely tuned awareness of what is required. Writers need to develop the necessary skills for communicating within stylistic conventions even when writing early drafts. Ensuring that ideas are accessible to the reader, that sentences are clear and concise and that longer sections of text are coherent need to be counterbalanced by the fact that the writing that you produce has to look and sound academic, whatever that might mean in your particular disciplinary area or areas.

The first step will be for you to revisit the kind of stylistic conventions that are likely to be familiar to doctoral level writers. These include *referencing techniques and formats*, the *amount of direct quotation* that is deemed acceptable and *bibliographical conventions*. Such issues will not be considered in this book, because of the difficulty of providing any form of meaningful non-disciplinary guidelines. A useful overview of referencing systems, formats, techniques and reference software is, however, provided by Grix & Watkins (2010).

There remains one convention that does need to be considered outside a disciplinary context, that of 'hedging' claims and arguments. In the following fabricated example from Chapter 2, the hedged expressions are underlined:

> _We suggest_ that the recent social unrest in rural communities in France _may possibly be due_ to problems which predate the recent arrival of wealthy Britons acquiring holiday homes.

According to Holliday (2002: 180) citing Dudley-Evans and St John (1998), there are two major functions of hedging. The first is 'distancing' the writer from the ideas that are being presented. The second function is 'softening' language:

> If a writer criticizes another by saying, 'Jones appears not to have under-stood the point I was making', the use of appears mitigates the criticism and is a politeness device rather than a distancing device.

Achieving an appropriate tone for claims is not an easy task. In Chapter 2, I presented some examples of how hedging can be taken too far. The more tentative the assertion, the less clear it can become. Even at doctoral level, writers can find it difficult to avoid an element of ambiguity.

Useful guidelines for hedging in research writing can be found on the websites of many UK universities. See, for example, the practical advice provided by Birkbeck College, University of London (Appendix 1). This is of particular interest since it includes ideas that appear at first glance to be contradictory. To hedge is said to involve using 'evasive or deliberately vague language' while at the same time being 'confidently uncertain'. What could this and other aspects of hedging mean in different academic disciplines? I received these responses from a group of PhD researchers in a recent thesis writing class:

Box 9.1. Hedging across disciplines

- In law there is a great need not to be woolly. But what about talking about someone who may or may not be guilty and you are not quite sure? You add 'allegedly', and this is hedging.
- The problem is that there is often an assumption that a claim is either yes or no. In journalism, this may be true (except for 'allegedly' perhaps?) But to say something is true and to suggest it may be true are two different propositions.

→

- *History is quite interesting because there are certain things that are not disputed. But there are certain 'facts' that we consider to be undisputed but in actually can be disputed. What illnesses did Richard III suffer from? Or Tutankhamen? There are all kinds of theories.*
- *Nothing can ever be beyond the shadow of a doubt in arts and humanities subjects.*

Being 'confidently uncertain' implies that you can hedge without being excessively vague and that hedging is a clear recognition that there may be some form of ambiguity or doubt associated with a statement that you are making. You can be 'confidently uncertain' with your position being that you may not be 100 per cent or even 50 per cent sure – you might instead be confident in one out of three or four instances. Whatever your discipline, you will need to think carefully about the force of the claims that you make and the language used to express them. Hyland (1995) points out that even in natural science disciplines, where precision and rigour are considered to be paramount, the expression of tentativeness through hedging is an essential component of academic style, one that is expected and valued by readers.

Style and stylishness

For some writers, expectations of academic style become confused with the notion of stylishness or elegance in writing. Sword (2012: 35) argues that 'elegant ideas deserve elegant expression' and sees disciplinary norms or expectations of style as actually working against this. She provides a useful image to bear in mind – that of an academic writer whose prose seems turgid and indigestible even though the arguments presented appear to be sound. In such cases, she claims that it is possible to predict with a certain degree of confidence that the text will have the following characteristics:

- an impersonal voice involving use of the passive rather than first-person singular 'I' or first-person plural 'we'
- failure to engage in a direct conversation with the reader (no use of 'you')
- strings of abstract nouns used to convey important information within sentences

In some ways, the debate about stylishness begun by Orwell (see Chapter 8) and continued by Sword has obscured the real issue. For most PhD theses elegant prose is desirable but not essential: the writer's most important task is surely to produce a text that meets expectations of clarity and coherence while looking and sounding 'academic'. When writers struggle to express themselves using academic language in a suitable style, guidelines for stylish or elegant prose do not provide a real solution. PhD supervisors who quote from Orwell may be well-intentioned, but they are arguably not providing the kind of advice that will really help.

It is also worth noting from the above quotation that this interpretation of elegance assumes adherence to certain conventions, such as the use of 'I' or 'we' rather than use of passive constructions. Unfortunately, writers in some disciplinary areas are denied this option. In the next section, we will consider in more detail what constitutes a suitable academic style across a number of disciplines, together with an analysis of what is acceptable in terms of difficulty and complexity as opposed to clarity of language.

Box 9.2. The 'Writer's Diet'

Helen Sword has created the 'Writer's diet' website (http://writersdiet.com/) as a tool for writers to assess the stylishness of their own writing. Upload a short section of text to see whether your writing is 'lean and mean' or 'flabby' and needing to go on some kind of diet. You will receive a rating for your use of verbs, nouns, prepositions, adjectives, adverbs and 'weak words' – for example, is/this/that. A full diagnosis gives advice in problem areas. The website is perhaps most useful as a means of comparing samples of your own writing *to check for stylistic consistency* since it will highlight sudden changes.

▶ Expectations of difficulty

> *I am wondering how to write this essay. Will I be intelligible or not? And if I am intelligible, does that mean that I have succeeded? And if I am not quite intelligible, or if I am unintelligible, then will that be a failure of communication?*

These lines provide the introduction to an article entitled 'The Values of Difficulty' by Judith Butler, an eminent American scholar and philosopher, in response to criticism of her particular style of writing. In fact, the article forms part of a collection of essays (Culler and Lamb 2003) in which writers from different disciplinary areas appear to defend themselves against accusations of obscurity, impenetrability and stylistic excess. In most cases this involves a discussion of the nature of clarity in writing and in particular the role of the reader in the process of meaningful communication. As McCumber, one of the contributors, puts it, 'My words are not clear until you have understood what I meant by them.'

Every now and then this kind of debate resurfaces. As far back as 1971, Andreski, a professor of sociology, published a book which focused on opaque and pretentious writing in the social sciences, which were then considered relatively new and arguably bent on attaining credibility in 'scientific' terms. Later, the issue came to the attention of a wider public with the publication of a hoax article (Sokal 1996) in which a physics professor at New York University deliberately submitted an article to the academic journal *Social Text*. His aim was to demonstrate that a certain kind of writing that looked credible on the surface and followed established disciplinary conventions in terms of style and presentation could be accepted for publication even when the content was fraudulent. As soon as the article had been published, Sokal revealed the hoax and denounced the journal for its inability to distinguish between genuine scholarship and nonsense hidden beneath a veil of imposing and resonant language.

During the same period, Dennis Dutton, the editor of the *Philosophy and Literature* journal, began a much publicized 'bad writing contest' (see Appendix 1). According to its instigator, the contest celebrates 'the most stylistically lamentable passages found in scholarly books and articles published in the last few years'. Judith Butler was the 1998 winner for one 94-word sentence containing 28 abstract nouns taken from a 1997 article entitled '*Further Reflections on the Conversations of Our Time,*' in the *Diacritics* scholarly journal.

Butler responded in a 1999 *New York Times* article entitled 'A "Bad Writer" Bites Back' in which she claimed that criticisms of her writing style might be politically motivated. At the same time, she acknowledged that there was a serious question to be considered, namely why certain ideas appear to require difficult and demanding language to get the message across. She also considered that it was unfair to ridicule one sentence taken out of context, an argument that many others might agree with.

More recently, in 2006, the author and academic Germaine Greer published an article in the *Guardian* in which she rejected criticism of her use of the expression 'the unsynthesised manifold' in an article intended for a general readership (Appendix 1). Of the hundreds of readers who commented on this online article, an approximate split of 60/40 per cent can be detected between those who felt offended by Greer's apparently condescending tone and those who supported her stance in defending the use of difficult language to express difficult ideas. An article written by Caroline Levine published in the *Times Higher Education Supplement* in 2007, 'The Art of the Impenetrable', also reflects both sides of the debate and provides a recognition of the fact that it has widened, no longer being the preserve of a few individual academics with scores to settle. More recently, Billig (2013) has devoted an entire book to the question of what constitutes poor quality writing in the social sciences. This author argues that there is an increasing tendency for researchers to self-promote through academic texts as academic life becomes more and more competitive. The overuse of jargon and excess of rhetoric are thus ways of making a writer's presence felt more strongly and their voice heard more loudly.

Further evidence of widening recognition of difficulty in academic writing can be found in the advice given to students in the most recent edition of the Chicago guide for students writing college papers:

> When you struggle to understand some academic writing (and you will), don't blame yourself, at least at first. Diagnose its sentences. If they have long subjects stuffed with abstract nouns, expressing new information, the problem is probably not your inability to read easily, but the writer's inability to write clearly. (Turabian et al. 2010: 137)

From the above examples, it can be seen that this longstanding debate is likely to continue and that there is a clear divide between two opposing camps. The arguments of the critics of stylistic excess (for example, Andreski 1971, Dutton 1999) could be summarized as follows:

1. Academic writers should aim to make complex ideas accessible in a jargon-free way.
2. Academic writers have a duty to promote clarity and coherence in their writing.
3. Experienced academic writers should set a good example so that the importance of clarity is seen to outweigh stylistic considerations.
4. Even the most difficult ideas can be expressed in relatively clear language.

Meanwhile, those who respond to such criticisms (see Culler and Lamb 2003) use a range of interesting counterarguments, some of which are listed here:

1. Clarity is relative (and it can be culturally determined).
2. Criticism of stylistic excess is often politically or personally motivated.
3. New ideas or ways of thinking ought not to be constrained by 'old' conventions.
4. Readers must share responsibility with writers for communicating meaning.
5. Difficulty is an essential part of critical thinking.

6. Conventional writing is 'dull'.
7. Difficult ideas can only be expressed by difficult language.
8. In some cultures, a sophisticated style is a mark of erudition.

▶ Classifying 'difficult texts'

The question arises as to how you should respond to the problems created by stylistically difficult texts when reading, and then how you can ensure that inappropriate stylistic excess is avoided when it is your turn to write. A useful first step might be to analyse the nature of the difficulty by dividing texts (for convenience) into distinct groups. Then, in each case, it will be useful to formulate guidelines for situations in which similar texts might need to be attempted. Your aim is always to enable stylistic considerations to be carefully balanced against the requirements for clarity, coherence and conciseness in a PhD thesis.

Group 1: Texts containing complex subject matter

The theoretical or abstract content of certain texts may give the impression that the language used to express ideas is stylistically difficult, but this may not be the case. The primary intention of the writer of such texts is to clarify knowledge and ideas either for a broader educated public or a more specialized readership. The writing may involve the use of technical expressions, but these do not appear to act as a smokescreen.

The language and structure of such texts are not the main source of their difficulty. If technical terminology is used, this is through necessity and not the result of stylistic excess. Guidelines for producing this type of text may include the following:

*   Make sure that key concepts are fully explained and explored within the text, in footnotes or by referring to another section of the thesis.
*   Avoid the use of technical jargon wherever possible. Provide an entry for technical terminology in a glossary if you expect that some of your readers may have problems understanding it.
*   Avoid the use of quotations which will add to the complexity of the text. Use only those quotations that will help to clarify the arguments being presented.
*   Pay particular attention to expectations and rules of coherence and text structure.

Group 2: Texts written in an idiosyncratic style

This category suggests that some writers adopt idiosyncrasies in their writing, consciously or unconsciously, in order to challenge the reader's way of thinking and acceptance of established stylistic conventions. This can apply to writers who deliberately choose unexpected words, use unusual descriptions, break up words ('geo-graphy', 'dis-ease'), invent new words or make frequent use of 'scare quotes' showing that certain expressions are being used in a nonstandard or an ironic way by adding either single or double inverted commas. The intention in such cases may be to shock the reader out of conventional thinking, to enliven prose that may otherwise appear dull or perhaps even to communicate more effectively in an unorthodox way. This consideration has sometimes been used as a defence of difficult writing. Judith Butler (1999) claims, for example, that she wants to challenge conventional thinking. In her view academic writing should be 'difficult and demanding' in order to 'question common sense'.

The following advice may be useful when dealing with 'idiosyncratic texts' as a reader or when you are considering integrating extracts from such texts or the style that they employ into your own writing:

- Although you may feel inspired to emulate the distinctive style of certain writers who have published extensively, there are clear dangers in producing texts that place great emphasis on challenging existing conventions. In the course of your academic career, you may develop your own clearly identifiable style. For a PhD thesis, existing conventions and reader expectations must be prioritized. This does not, however, imply that you are forced to write in a highly constrained way, adopting a style that may feel completely alien to you.
- You will need to take great care when including extracts from 'idiosyncratic texts' written by other authors within your own work. Ensure that you provide a clear interpretation of the arguments being presented: it may be unwise to assume that your interpretation will automatically be understood or shared by your readers.
- Devices such as 'scare quotes' need to be used in moderation. Frequent use will slow down readers, leading them to question and think too carefully about every single concept that is highlighted in this way. If this is not your intention, remove sets of quotation marks that are unnecessary.

Group 3: Translated texts
Texts which are translated from another language into English present a particular set of problems, especially in cases where the content is quite abstract. Such texts may sound uncomfortable in English despite the best efforts of translators.

According to Steiner (1975) each language 'maps the world differently'. As a result, certain terms may lose their intended meaning in the first language when translated. Wierzbicka (1997) has examined a range of more abstract terms across several languages and shown how their meaning may vary across cultures. She notes that 'philosophers, political scientists, and students of law are usually aware of the untranslatability of more or less technical concepts such as "bail", "warrant", "custody", "solipsism", "determinism", "parliament", "oath", and "democracy"'. Her study focuses on some nontechnical concepts expressed by English words such as 'freedom', which she explains in some detail are understood differently in Latin, English, Russian and Polish.

Further problems arise when writers are highly idiosyncratic in the first language in terms of style and choice of words. This may be virtually impossible to render effectively in another language. While not all translated texts present such levels of difficulty, it is useful to consider the following guidelines for using any translated extracts that need to be incorporated within your own PhD thesis:

- You will need to take steps to satisfy yourself that the translated extract is faithful to the original version. If there is any doubt in this matter, it is better not to include the extract.
- If any words or expressions in the extract are unclear or ambiguous, convey your own interpretation to the reader as clearly and as concisely as possible. This can be in the form of a footnote if you prefer to avoid digressions in your text.

Group 4: 'Intentionally difficult' texts

In this category, we can place texts that show deliberate ambiguity or camouflaging of a lack of ideas by over-complex language. While idiosyncratic writing may be *intentional* in shocking the reader out of complacent thinking, or *unintentional* in its difficulty, texts in the 'intentionally difficult' category may deliberately sacrifice clarity in order to give an impression of sophistication. The following may be some of the features of such texts:

- long sentences
- complexity of grammatical structure of sentences – for example, those containing multiple clauses or those where the subject is separated from the verb
- the choice of obscure words to convey simple meanings
- abstraction that appears to cover up lack of substantial ideas
- overuse of unnecessary 'scare quotes' or words in parentheses
- 'name-dropping' – overuse of source references to create a positive impression

- excessive use of repetition, redundancy, side-tracking and exemplification
- illogical sequencing of facts or ideas

One writer who might be placed in this category is the anthropologist Stephen Tyler. Paul Stoller has compared his writing to 'a mangrove swamp' containing 'a profusion of Greek terms ... a profusion of neologisms ... a profusion of ironic syntax' (Stoller 1991: 105, cited by Lukas 1999: 10). Tyler's initial response (in an interview with Lukas) was that he does not consider his own writing particularly difficult but maintains that it might perhaps be difficult for those who expect the kind of writing that occurs in most anthropological texts. He goes on to claim that if most readers were able to understand him, he would consider that he had failed as a writer and that if writers are allowed to challenge other conventions, then conventions of clarity and coherence should not be exempt from this process. When some writers say to themselves, 'I want to write in a difficult way', they should in his view be respected for doing so.

If a writer claims that deliberate difficulty has a subversive purpose, we are therefore led to assume that there is a certain kind of integrity behind this way of thinking. However, there is some evidence that academics in some fields resort to this kind of writing in order to gain credibility and even become publishable. One entrant in the previously mentioned 'bad writing contest' (cited by Myers 2005) believes that getting published in many journals means:

> flinging the jargon, toeing the party line (which is somewhere to the left of gibberish), and quoting the usual suspects (Benjamin, Foucault, Derrida, Said, Jameson, Butler, etc.). I'm often appalled by my own writing, but since jargon, rather than substance, gains a publication, I succumb to verbiage.

Every discipline creates its own specialist terms. However, it is possible to camouflage obvious, common-sense observations with jargon that suggests something deeper than the actual meaning of what is being conveyed. It is not clear whether Butler, Tyler and other authors would reject some kinds of writing on the grounds of stylistic excess and, if so, what criteria they would use. It may not always be easy to distinguish what is deliberately opaque from the idiosyncratic writing that was identified in the second category. The question raised by examples within this fourth category is whether it would be worth making the effort to make sense of them at all and whether we should just accept that fact that some writers are happy to exclude a large number of readers, thus limiting the possibility of debating the issues presented.

For PhD thesis writers, stylistic excess is not a realistic option. Rephrasing problem texts, instead, so that they are expressed more clearly can be a useful guiding exercise. Consider, for example, the following fabricated example. What changes could be made?

Box 9.3. Simplifying a complex text

The augmented momentum and accompanying interactive dynamics of business activity in urban areas engender transformational processes in the labour market that can catalyse action potentials in emerging niches of opportunity in a varied multiplicity of sectors.

- *Identify complex structures*: one long complex sentence can be converted into two simple statements, such as 'The increase in business activity in urban areas can transform the labour market. This in turn can provide new opportunities in different sectors'.
- *Avoid jargon*: find substitute words or expressions for 'catalyse action potentials'.
- *Convert abstract nouns and adjectives*: 'transformational processes' becomes 'transform'.
- *Simplify abstract nouns and adjectives*: 'the augmented momentum' becomes 'the increase'.
- *Reduce redundancy*: 'the augmented momentum and accompanying interactive dynamics of business activity' become 'the increase in business activity'.

Box 9.4. A revised version of the complex text

The increase in business activity in urban areas can transform the labour market. This in turn can provide new opportunities in different sectors.

If a single problematic sentence can be improved in five different ways, it is evident that longer pieces of text may benefit from this kind of approach. The sentence clarity checklist provided in Chapter 8 may be used for this purpose when editing and revising a first draft text.

Group 5: Mixed-styles texts

Some writers appear to be inconsistent in their use of academic style, seemingly switching in and out of 'different tones of voice'. This is surprisingly common and may involve:

- the inclusion of complex or inappropriate quotations from other authors
- the inclusion of complex or ambiguous concept diagrams in an otherwise clear text
- passages of narrative which are accessible to the reader but that contrast with passages of analysis which are less so

For an interesting example of this type of text, see Chapter 2 of Zygmunt Bauman's 'Liquid Love' (2003) – in which the author discusses ways in which 'virtual and non-virtual proximity' have changed places, with the virtual variety becoming stronger as people all over the world make use of mobile technology. In this text, passages of straightforward narrative alternate with denser, more complex paragraphs of analysis. An effective strategy might be for the reader to consider the narrative passages first, proceeding then to the more difficult paragraphs in which the voices of other writers join in the debate. However, this would mean changing the order in which the paragraphs are intended to be read.

What can be learned from the five categories of 'difficult text' concerning the development of your own academic style? I suggest the following:

- *Reader expectations are paramount*: Writers should certainly be allowed and encouraged to adopt a style with which they are comfortable, but the expectations of readers cannot be ignored if effective communication is to be achieved.
- *Expectations of style may vary*: If you are working in more than one disciplinary area with doctoral supervisors from those different areas, it is possible that you may receive conflicting messages concerning acceptable style. Ultimately, you must decide in consultation with all the people concerned – will I adopt style A or style B?
- *Adherence to a particular style needs to be consistent*: Any changes in style will have to be fully justified. In the case of the Bauman text referred to above, the change in style does help make the arguments clearer through illustration. There is a judicious switch from a more complex academic style to a simple narrative. However, if there is no clear rationale for changing the writing style, this can confuse and irritate readers in equal measure.
- *Stylistic excess is counterproductive*: Think carefully, for example, before adding a quotation in order to impress your readers. If a quotation

helps to clarify meaning or adds weight to an argument, then it can be included. If it distracts from your message, leave it out. Think carefully also about the use of the words used to express the most important ideas that you wish to convey. If your ideas are hidden behind a veil of stylistic excess, you will not only make the reader's task more difficult but also (perhaps) give a distinct impression that the resonance of your rhetoric is a means of disguising a lack of ideas.

In conclusion, you should indeed have a degree of freedom to make decisions about your preferred writing style. However, you will need to show at all times that you are aware of stylistic conventions and the kind of language that academics in your field would normally use. You should not feel imprisoned by the constraints of stylistic conventions. Consider them as a guide to help you achieve a shared language between yourself and other academic writers in your field. They should never be called upon to justify the production of turgid, impenetrable prose.

Action Points

1. Familiarize yourself with the workings of cross-disciplinary academic style conventions, such as 'hedging'. Familiarize yourself also with discipline-specific style conventions. Consult any style guides that are available in your area, and be aware of how style is used in well-regarded 'model' texts.
2. In your reading, respond to stylistically difficult texts by analysing the causes.
3. In your writing, ensure that inappropriate stylistic excess is avoided. Checklists such as those provided in Chapters 8 and 9 can help in this respect.
4. Check written chapters for stylistic inconsistencies. Once you have settled on a suitable balance between clarity and style that works for you and for your readers, check your work for stylistic consistency. Be prepared to justify any changes in style that may not conform to reader expectations.
5. Make a note to remind yourself to make any necessary adjustments when chapters are being edited.

10 Completing a First Draft

This chapter

- *considers the challenges of producing a first draft of 80,000–100,000 words*
- *compares the experience of writing down ideas for the first time with the editing process where the aim is to revise, correct and polish*

▶ The basic writing cycle

So far in this handbook we have discussed the planning of research writing in terms of its structure (Chapter 6) and the ways in which productive writing routines can be developed (Chapter 7). The delicate balance between clarity, coherence and academic style has also been explored (in Chapters 8 and 9). Structure, clarity, coherence and (to a lesser extent) style are all important elements of first draft writing, which is arguably the most demanding task for any research writer. In contrast, many would argue that text editing is a smoother and more enjoyable process. The author James Michener shares this point of view and is often quoted as claiming to be less able as a writer than as a rewriter.

I find writing the first draft of any academic text to be a painful, messy and time-consuming process. The primary aim is to commit all of the content and the argumentation to screen or paper in a structured and coherent manner. Once a significant amount of content has been written down in some form, the process of reallocating sections of text can begin. You can, for example, plan Chapter 3 but then realize that it lacks a certain amount of substance; it can be reallocated as a section or subsection within Chapter 4. You may scrutinize your plan for Chapter 5 and conclude that the text will be straightforward to write; it then grows steadily in size to such an extent that you have to consider dividing it into two or three new chapters, or sections that will fit into existing chapters.

This process of reallocating text forms an integral part of the first draft writing process. The reason for this is simple: while you are attempting to put into practice an initial plan, you will discover that your thinking is likely to change. For this reason it seems inadvisable and possibly even dangerous to work single-mindedly on one chapter until it has reached the point where it has been completed and thoroughly polished. By the time you have finished (for example) Chapter 5, you may be forced to reconsider the content of earlier chapters. Many research writers fail to appreciate the need for flexibility at this stage: as your thinking changes, so will your writing.

The problem can be exacerbated by the demands of readers, whether they are publishing editors, PhD supervisors or your colleagues. A long first draft may not be the preferred option for certain readers who would like you to submit individual chapters in a manageable and orderly way. In such circumstances, it may be tempting to try to perfect certain chapters even when being aware of the potential pitfalls of this type of approach.

Other important elements within the cycle of first draft writing will include the following:

- how to evaluate a first draft once it has been written
- how to receive quality feedback
- how to vary the sources of feedback
- how to re-plan and revise text in response to feedback
- how to edit an acceptable first draft

Later sections of this chapter will examine all of these in greater detail.

▶ Managing reader expectations

Arguably, one of the most important principles in first draft writing is the concept of 'managing the expectations of readers', a principle briefly introduced in Chapter 6. This is an intuitive process for many skilled and experienced research writers. As a writer, you attempt to enter the mind of the reader, trying to think consistently about how readers will understand your text and then writing with such readers in mind. This appears to be a fundamental aspect of becoming a skilled creator of lengthy research texts. In the case of a PhD thesis, it will not just be the reader's problem if your text is inaccessible. If you are unable to connect with your reader, the thesis may have to be substantially revised or completely rewritten.

How can you anticipate what readers will expect and then successfully manage those expectations? An immediate problem is that expectations may vary across disciplines and perhaps among individuals within a single disciplinary area. However, within the UK academic culture, a set of core expectations can be identified, including the following:

- the production of a carefully written *abstract* telling the reader 'this is what you can expect when you start to read this work'
- the production of a well-crafted *table of contents* that will guide readers through the overall structure and sequencing of your work
- clear section and subsection *headings*
- careful attention being paid to the *introductory sections of chapters, concluding sections* and *interim conclusions*
- careful attention being paid to *signposting* within the rest of the text

All of these indicate to the reader that 'these are the directions in which I will lead you'. Your readers may be experts in their field, but they will still require some guidance in this respect.

Signalling and signposting: topic sentences

Even within a first draft, you will need to consider how you will signal your intentions to the reader through the means of clear signposts. There are two well-established ways of signalling your intentions: the first involves the use of *topic sentences*, propositions that are explained and explored within a paragraph, while the second consists of the use of explicit *discourse markers* specially selected to link pieces of text together. I will argue that the use of topic sentences is generally the preferable option on the grounds that such sentences are connected to text structure, to paragraphing and to underlying coherence. Formulaic discourse markers or 'linking expressions', on the other hand, tend to be markers of structure only (see Chapter 8 for further discussion of this).

An interesting example of how topic sentences can be made to work effectively is to be found in these extracts from the opening chapter of a first draft PhD thesis written by a historian:

Box 10.1. The Rev Isaac and Mrs Ann Taylor: Family, Faith, Profession

Paragraph 1: In 1778 when Isaac Taylor II met his future wife Ann Martin, the daughter of a pawnbroker, he was 19 years old, apprenticed as an engraver to his father having been unable to fulfil his ambition to become a minister, and engaged to a member of a prominent nonconformist

→

family, 10 years his senior. All other information surrounding the origins of this successful nonconformist literary family, the Taylors of Ongar, were excluded by family members with the exception of ...

Paragraph 2: In the mid to late nineteenth century as part of their literary output members of the Taylor family produced a series of autobiographies, biographies and recollections for journals and magazines. These writings have subsequently been used to ...

Paragraph 3: Above all the memoirs reveal much new information on Mrs Ann Martin Taylor, whose literary reputation has been constrained by the stereotypical portrait constructed of her as a conservative, evangelical literary figure based on the limited information available in published family memoirs....

End of Paragraph 3: From the information now available through the memoirs, combined with other primary source materials including letters and church records, a much more complex and intriguing picture emerges from the generalized stereotypes that have been constructed around the Taylor family of Ongar.

Paragraph 4: For both Rev Isaac Taylor II and Mrs Ann Taylor the early years of their lives spent in London provided seminal experiences that, it will be argued, had a significant influence on the development of the family ethos and their literary careers. During Rev Isaac Taylor's early life....

Well-crafted topic sentences guide the reader clearly and effectively. They tend to appear at the very beginning of paragraphs as a clear statement of intent. This is the case in the abbreviated sample text above concerning the literary output of the Taylors of Ongar:

Paragraph 1 opens with the only definite public information that exists concerning the Taylor family. This leads into a discussion of why this is the case and how other information has been made widely available.

Paragraph 2 draws attention to a particular set of memoirs produced by the family. This leads into discussion of how these memoirs throw new light on their literary activities.

Paragraph 3 highlights one particular aspect of the information that is now available from the Taylor memoirs – the literary output of Mrs Ann Taylor. This leads on to the claim that a more complex appreciation of her work is required, questioning the rather stereotypical portrait produced by other writers.

Paragraph 4 turns our attention to the early life of the two main protagonists – Isaac and Ann Taylor. The narrative then continues along this track.

Note how each topic sentence carefully guides the reader, providing a clear starting point for the development of each piece of the narrative and accompanying analysis. Paragraph beginnings achieve this effect throughout the whole of the chapter. However, the most interesting claim, that 'a much more complex and intriguing picture emerges from the generalized stereotypes' appears at the end of a paragraph rather than at the beginning. This is not uncommon in a well-structured and coherent text. It seems that topic sentences do not need to appear at the beginning of a paragraph to achieve the desired levels of clarity within a text. Readers may reasonably expect either alternative.

When important information or arguments are placed in the middle of even a short piece of text, however, they will tend to be less noticeable. As a result, the text will usually be less easy to understand and its 'flow' will be broken as the reader begins to re-read sections containing important information that has been missed. When topic sentences appear in places that can be expected, the reader will be more likely to stay on track. When topic sentences are hidden in unexpected places, the coherence of the text in the mind of the reader can be greatly affected.

The power of topic sentences lies in their ability to glue text together, to help us to understand and to help us to anticipate where a text is going. If at some point we lose direction, it means the glue is probably spread too thinly. If the glue is strong enough, it will carry the reader, enabling them to follow and read very quickly; where the glue does not exist, the reader will be forced to re-read many times. By pulling out and highlighting the topic sentences, a reader can make sense of a piece of text, even one where complex ideas are being presented and discussed. In addition, if we use topic sentences as a framework, we can build up our own writing so that coherence is achieved. First draft writing is about content and committing ideas to paper or screen, but it is also about achieving coherence. We cannot leave issues related to coherence to be dealt with only during the editing stage.

▶ Drafting and redrafting

> *I keep going back to my drafts and thinking about changing them.* (1st-year PhD student, law)

How many drafts could be considered too many for the same piece of writing? While recognizing that certain sections will be more difficult and that we will have to redraft more, is there a limit to this? Is there a point where we need to call a halt, and how do we recognize when we have reached that point? Such questions require careful consideration, as evidence suggests a strong link between the processes of both drafting and redrafting and becoming blocked as a writer (see Chapter 11). Your initial plans for a chapter and your writing targets can seem very distant when you find yourself drafting the same piece of text four or five times without a sense of real progress. If a supervisor were to say, 'this is your fourth draft, but I want you to do a fifth one', I think it would be reasonable to ask to start writing something else and to return to the text in question later. In fact, most PhD supervisors would be unlikely to insist on a fifth draft, except in exceptional circumstances.

Although this may seem at first sight to be a contradiction, redrafting text as you write is an important part of the first draft process. This process tends to be cyclical rather than linear: only in rare cases will just one attempt be enough. Two or three redrafts can be considered normal. Anything beyond this requires careful consideration and justification.

Effective first draft writing *involves the gradual construction of an entire text rather than joining together a series of well-constructed and polished texts.* An alternative approach might involve producing a first draft of each chapter in turn, redrafting in response to reader feedback, progressing to the next chapter and repeating the process. Although it is possible to write in this way, failing to consider the text as a whole can result in a lack of coherence between chapters, with different parts of the thesis becoming disconnected from others. The most productive way of preventing this from happening is to put in place a system for careful monitoring of the text as it grows in size.

▶ Monitoring progress

Keeping a writing journal or diary
Gradually building a text without losing coherence can be a complicated process and may require additional support. Some writers believe that producing *a reflective writing journal* can help to provide this. How might it work in practice?

> *I write about the problems that I am facing. If I get lost, for example, I have found it useful because sometimes I become more aware about what I am doing, where my research topic is going, how my point of view differs from that of my supervisor. So it is a kind of therapy.*

This writer and others say to themselves: 'This was my thinking on this particular day', followed by a discussion of the progress that has been made and questions that need to be addressed. Recording such impressions can help many research writers. When I started my own PhD thesis more than 20 years ago, I found the early chapters difficult to write. Subsequently, I travelled abroad to collect data as part of a qualitative study and was advised to keep a data collection journal. This worked as an effective means of pulling together all of the different types of data collected from interviews, observations of teaching and focus groups. When I returned from fieldwork data collection, I decided to continue the habit of keeping a reflective journal to record my progress while writing in an attempt to keep myself on track. Whenever I felt blocked, confused or perplexed during first draft writing, I would read this journal carefully so that I could try to establish how I had managed to reach the blocking point. Occasionally, I would be able to work out an exact route, retrace my steps and begin to plot an alternative. For this process to work effectively, I needed to exercise a degree of self-discipline when recording events or pieces of analysis within the journal.

Some people have this kind of self-discipline naturally. A few years ago after the death of my mother, my sister and I discovered boxes of diaries going back to the early 1950s, when I was a young child. Having read through them, I found the reconnection to be almost instant – everything was there. The diaries brought back vividly the daily routine and problems of life in the immediate post-war period. My mother's concerns and reflections were of their time. For example, buying a washing machine or a television was an important event and involved the visits of admiring neighbours and friends. Certain entries were puzzling: for instance, I found it difficult to understand the constant washing of floors and walls, cleaning of curtains and carpets. The carefully recorded visits of the chimneysweep then reminded me of why these activities were so frequent and so necessary.

Reading documents such as these, it is possible to reconnect to a previous period of time and a previous way of thinking. Having the discipline to put thoughts down on paper in this way can result in a powerful and useful document later on when memory has begun to distort the past. My mother kept diaries with no intended readership apart from herself, although many members of our family have subsequently benefited from reading them. In my case, I decided to keep a journal – different from my concept of a diary in that there would be at least one other intended reader. From time to time, my supervisor asked to see this document, as it provided her with a useful means of picking up the thread of my progress. On one occasion she went so far as to make the tongue-in-cheek suggestion that the journal might eventually be of more interest than the PhD thesis itself. Unfortunately, very few extracts survive. One is reproduced below:

Box 10.2. Extract from a reflective writing journal

I know chapter 4 is far too long. I will perhaps be able to shorten it when chapter 5 is written and the less relevant parts of chapter 4 can then shrink almost to nothing. A lot of quotes could perhaps be transferred into Chapter 5 as I work through the main issues which come out from the data. The main question is: is it readable? Or is it just like a list of events? If I shorten it too much, will I have to have long appendices with transcripts of everything? It's very difficult for me to decide all of this because I can't really stand back from it.

My journal entries tended to focus on problem areas. They included my concerns about certain chapters which did not seem to make any sense, my uncertainties concerning whether I should break up larger chapters or not, my frustration when reaching apparent dead ends. These musings are very revealing when I look back on the experience of writing a PhD thesis. Seen from a distance of more than 20 years, the process might appear to be seamless. It is easy to forget the pain and effort required to complete certain chapters. When I re-read these journal notes, the reality of the situation returns and I remember my struggles with chapters 4 and 5 in particular.

A reflective writing journal is worth careful consideration because it can be an important document in its own right. It records why you make certain choices at certain points in time. In producing a long text many such choices will have to be made. Do you need a more substantial chapter 1? Should you continue with chapter 3 and put aside for the moment considerations of chapter 5? If you can write down all your thinking in this way, you may be able to justify your decisions more easily and more effectively, especially the major decisions related to reallocating content within the first draft.

As Wolcott (1990) states, writing is very much about clarifying thinking and is not just the end product of thinking. If you can develop a parallel narrative at a metacognitive level, thinking about your thinking and thinking about your writing, this can be of significant help. One other consequence of monitoring progress in this way may be that it may help you to achieve a certain amount of distance from your work and to establish more clearly your own position.

Finally, a research journal can encourage useful critical self-evaluation (see Chapter 7). This needs to be considered carefully because there is always a danger that you can go too far and that latent perfectionist tendencies could turn the monitoring process into a purely negative exercise. One of the most common reasons for non-completion of this long piece of writing is the desire to achieve a perfect first draft. Naturally, this can never be achieved.

Critical self-evaluation needs therefore to be justified and rationalized. If you fail to provide a balanced picture of where you are at a particular moment, the consequences can be serious. Every writer at some point has thought aloud, 'I know that my work lacks real worth, and I also know that someone somewhere is writing something much better. My project did seem interesting but no longer does, and maybe no one will read the results of my work'. Chapter 11 will address such issues and their consequences.

Blogging

Another alternative to a research journal might be a PhD writing blog, typified by an example produced by a researcher at the London School of Economics (see Appendix 1). Blogs that you produce and those written by other researchers can be very inspiring. There are many potential advantages according to these PhD thesis writers:

> Blogging can be a release from all the structural pressures corroding the creative impulse of academic writing.... Waiting for the organic moment of inspiration when deadlines loom can be unreliable.
>
> Blogging becomes a vehicle for intellectual exploration and a reflection on writing.
>
> As well as your own blog, other specialist blogs where you can get into the conversation can be useful. You can take your concerns into this type of forum using the comments sections, sharing them with others. An active Facebook page can almost serve as a kind of problem corner. There are lots of people out there who have exactly the same problem as you, and you will also find expertise.

There are obvious differences between a reflective journal and a blog. People will read and will respond to a blog; after all, it is a public document. Its ability to be interactive also has considerable advantages if you would like feedback on your writing, assuming that you receive encouraging as well as more critical comments. A colleague who recently set up her own blog on an unrelated theme reports that the enthusiastic response has encouraged her to such an extent that for the first time, writing has become an enjoyable and rewarding experience. A reflective journal or diary is a more personal document in which you talk to yourself and possibly one or two others. With a blog, talking to yourself takes place in a public arena. It is a way of rationalizing what you are doing with the addition of feedback, even from people who you do not know. According to one researcher, 'You have enormous freedom because you can choose your topic yourself and write the way you want to write'.

The problem about creating your own blog is that it takes time and effort which could be directed elsewhere. However, with your own blog, there is no particular requirement to post regularly – but just when you feel like it and have time. Some people go on 'blog holidays' and return after a few months refreshed.

Finally, it is worth noting that writing on social media sites can also be a source of encouragement according to this PhD student writer:

> *On my Facebook page I write about where I am having difficulties. As some people who respond are not specialists, you end up having to explain things. And this helps you fine-tune or pick through whatever it is that is going on. It's not a diary or a blog, but it is a way of making your ideas public without thinking that it has to be academic writing.*

▶ Writing and editing

In the final section of this chapter, we consider the differences between first draft writing and chapter editing. A typical first draft writing cycle might look like this:

- planning the overall structure of chapters
- writing sections of an initial first draft
- printing out
- reflecting on the printout and obtaining feedback from other sources
- reallocating text where necessary, filling gaps and making cuts
- producing a 'final' version of the first draft

The advice of the novelist John Steinbeck can be of assistance when we are attempting to separate the processes of first draft writing and editing:

> *Write freely and as rapidly as possible and throw the whole thing on paper. Never correct or rewrite till the whole thing is down.* (Steinbeck & Wallsten 1989)

In other words, a first draft can contain flaws, and there is no requirement to edit text carefully before moving from one section or chapter to another.

To what extent is Steinbeck's straightforward advice relevant in an academic writing context? You might begin by identifying the underlying narrative within your research. The story of how you planned your data collection, how you collected it and what you discovered could be one strand. The story of how you considered different theoretical frameworks to help make sense of your research and how you chose one of them might be another. Arguably, there is some element of narrative in each important aspect of a research project. Committing the events of this narrative to paper and clearly and simply conducting the accompanying analysis are your tasks.

If you follow Steinbeck's advice, there is no need at this stage to worry unduly about details of academic style, minor points of uncertainty (just put a question mark) or even minor factual errors: these can be checked at a later stage, as long as they are highlighted. For example, if a date is uncertain, write yourself a note that says, 'I need to check this'. If you spend a great deal of time checking references in detail, you could easily become distracted from the main task of getting your ideas down on paper.

Distinguishing between the details that you do have to worry about and those that you do not is an important first draft writing task. Unfortunately, not everyone will agree with this distinction. My experience with my own PhD supervisor is that she had very strict views about punctuation. If I submitted a chapter to her and asked for feedback, this would invariably focus on my misuse of commas. My task was to convince her that the final version of the text would be polished and error free, suitably punctuated throughout. Once she had that confidence, she tended to focus more on the content of what I had written.

If a PhD supervisor has never seen a final version of a text written by you, such concerns are understandable. You will need to provide reassurance, perhaps by showing another text that has been finalized and (preferably) published. An important conversation with a supervisor involves ensuring that both of you are clear about expectations not just of the first draft but also of the final draft that you will submit.

Another useful approach is to respond to reader feedback as follows: 'Thank you for telling me this. I will not implement all of these changes immediately but will consider them at the editing stage.' This reassurance will usually be enough to show that you are aware of problem areas and have noted them carefully. In fact, the problem is not usually the nature of errors, but the way in which writers and readers respond to them. If you can produce a polished first draft in terms of language accuracy and style, this is commendable. However, when problems appear, you will need to convince yourself and your readers that the fundamental aim of the first draft is to get the content right.

To summarize, 'writing freely' within a first draft process can mean:

- telling a story clearly and simply
- not worrying about minor factual errors at this stage
- not immediately revising grammar, spelling and punctuation
- not worrying excessively about paragraph length
- not over-worrying about conciseness or stylistic considerations, though an awareness of academic style does need to be built into the text

'Writing freely' within a first draft needs, however, to take account of:

- inclusion of key arguments and counterarguments with supporting evidence
- exploration of key concepts
- coherence of argumentation

Failing to address coherence issues at this early stage will have consequences. If ideas are expressed in a less than coherent way, there is even a danger that when you re-read them you will fail to understand them. As an aid to coherence, you will need to build in carefully crafted topic sentences and other forms of signalling. Although you can add detail later, you also need to include all of the key arguments and counterarguments and to explore and define key terminology, making sure that it is used consistently. Terminology is not a matter of detail: you need to make sure in your choice of words that you are conveying the message that you want to get across.

A dissenting view comes from a 1st-year PhD researcher in response to these recommendations concerning which areas to prioritize:

> *If accuracy of language is not tackled early on in the process, there will be a real problem when it comes to writing up. Some students take up to three years to get their language level up to the point where they can write an acceptable final draft.*

The response might be that there is a clear difference between flagging up problems and having to make corrections immediately. Where a writer commits language errors that impede coherence and comprehensibility, then that is a serious matter. If a writer is making punctuation errors which do not affect understanding of the text, that person has a choice – to address the punctuation problems immediately, with the risk of being distracted from the main task, or to come to an agreement with the readers to deal with this later. It may even be the case that a proofreader or a copyeditor can do part of this work when the final version is produced.

Note also that the first draft writing process does not absolve you from doing any of the following:

1. *Writing aimlessly without a plan or an awareness of where the text is heading*
   Your overall plan articulated through documents such as the table of contents, abstract, monthly schedule or reflective journal needs to be readily accessible at all times. Many writers also find individual chapter plans pinned prominently near the computer screen to be helpful. At regular intervals during writing, the question that you will need to ask yourself is, 'Am I still on track'?

2. *Omitting introductory or concluding sections to chapters*
   These are an essential element of first draft writing. For further discussion of the issues involved in creating high-quality introductions and conclusions, see Chapter 6.

3. *Confusing your own ideas with those of other authors*
   In a text as lengthy as a PhD thesis, this can be a major cause of loss of coherence. References need to be integrated into a first draft in such a way as to create no ambiguity concerning ownership of the ideas that are being presented. Precise referencing markers such as 'according to Benson (1993)' or 'Benson (1993) claims that' are nearly always preferable to adding a name and date at the end of a paragraph or combination of sentences within a paragraph. In a worst case scenario, you may find when you re-read the text that you are no longer certain how some of the ideas originated.

4. *Preventing yourself from re-reading what you have written as the text grows*
   Re-reading is an important element in the first draft process, as is redrafting to correct imbalances within the text. A first draft of any chapter within a PhD thesis can never be regarded as a linear process, nor should it ever be confused with a rough draft written in a continuous burst of activity. First draft writing is a complex, non-intuitive process that involves a gradual accumulation of pieces of written text that may need to be revised to fit together as a coherent whole. The final, polished version of the text will come later, when feedback has been taken into account and careful editing has taken place. In the meantime, the completion of an entire first draft means that you have taken your most significant step towards achieving success. It is an occasion to be celebrated almost as much as the submission of the printed final version itself.

Action Points

1. Build <u>carefully crafted topic sentences</u> into your first draft writing to help manage the expectations of your readers.
2. Consider keeping <u>a writing journal</u> to help you keep track of your progress.
3. Consider starting <u>a writing blog</u> to help you communicate with other writers who have progressed to a similar stage. A blog may also enable you to learn from the experience of others who are several stages ahead.
4. Make sure that you appreciate the clear differences between <u>producing first draft texts and editing texts</u>. Focus on extensive, detailed editing once a first draft has been produced rather than during first draft production.

11 Motivating Yourself to Write

This chapter

- *considers the nature of writer's block, its causes and consequences*
- *presents a range of strategies that can either enable you to pre-empt blockages or that will help you deal with them effectively*
- *offers advice on coping with situations that involve the rejection of written work*

▶ Writing is more than just a technical exercise

A PhD student once told me about the occasion when she felt so blocked in her writing that she decided to give up her entire research project:

> I wrote to my supervisor: 'I'm giving up and going back to my own country. I apologize.' He replied: 'Sorry? You can't say these kinds of things by email in this way. We need to talk about this in person.'

When they met the next day, the advice given by the supervisor was to begin a fixed routine: get up at the same time, go to the gym, write for a few hours, have lunch, continue to write and then stop. Every day the routine should be the same. He also arranged a new office where all of this writing could take place. The student began to make some progress with her writing. The situation was eventually saved.

The experience of many writers suggests that a regular routine of this kind can be helpful and in this particular case, it worked well thanks to the quick thinking and sensitivity of the supervisor. The writer was feeling isolated, demotivated and homesick. Some words of understanding and simple practical advice were required from someone who realized that writing a long text is as much a psychological as a technical exercise.

However, there are occasions where such simple solutions are not enough. It is possible to reach a stage where you begin to think, 'What I am writing has little value or no value. I am wasting my time and other people's time.' This is the point when you really begin to entertain thoughts of giving up. It seems that self-motivation is not just linked to self-discipline and to the degree of success achieved in the management of the whole PhD project, but also linked to underlying beliefs concerning the quality of the work and perceptions of your own abilities. Goleman (1996) goes further, arguing that self-motivation can be broken down into qualities such as resilience and optimism. These, arguably, are also key components of a more general 'emotional intelligence' (see Chapter 5), which many believe is an important indicator of success.

This chapter will consider the importance of self-motivation, self-discipline, self-belief and other psychological aspects of writing. Rather than consider all of these in turn, however, the approach taken will be to look at what happens when things go wrong and to seek to identify solutions which will enable you to keep writing whatever the circumstances.

▶ The nature of writer's block

When the ability to manage the writing process, or self-belief, or optimism and resilience fail, the result can be the appearance of what is often known as the 'first draft wall', a form of writer's block. Some writers, such as Nelson (1993), argue that writer's block can contain a strong positive element:

> *Writers tend to think of themselves in a number of ways, all bad. They are, so they think, lazy undisciplined shirkers, failures, cowardly frauds, good-for-nothings. The list of negatives stretches into cold infinity.... Being temporarily unable to write, however, or for that matter to perform any creative endeavour, is not a bad thing in itself. Properly interpreted a block is the best thing that can happen to a writer. Resistance is a vital regulator of the creative process because it obliges us to suspend our plans and reconsider the nature of our relation to the creative forces.*

In other words, writer's block appears to be part of the natural process of writing, a means of saying to a writer, 'stop before you go any further, and think about what you are doing'. Applying the brakes from time to time is thus seen to be a necessary procedure. However, this view does not offer a great deal of comfort to those who believe that they have hit a solid wall that they cannot pass through, climb over or circumvent. Nelson herself admits that there is a misconception of writer's block as a neutral state.

The truth is that this is no passive condition. It is an aggressive reaction, a loud shout from the unconscious calling the attention to the fact that something is out of adjustment. The block itself is not the problem. It is a signal to adjust the way we approach our work…. Writers who find themselves unable to produce have made a choice not to write but they do not experience it as choice. (1993: 2)

Clearly, it can be useful to recognize the different manifestations of writer's block, consider its causes and explore possible solutions. Writer's block means different things to different people and is often portrayed by writers in works of literature. In Albert Camus' novel 'La Peste', written in 1947, a town in Algeria is cut off by the bubonic plague, and the people inside gradually realize that that they will all die. They begin to prepare for death in a dignified way. Among them, Joseph Grand is a civil servant who has always aspired to be a great novelist. He announces to his colleague, 'What I really want, doctor, is this. On the day the manuscript reaches the publisher I want him to stand up—after he's read it through, of course—and say to his staff: "Gentlemen, hats off!" … So you see, … it's got to be flawless.'

Grand takes extraordinary pains to bring his work to perfection, with evenings and whole weekends 'spent on just one word'. He dies having written just one sentence, beyond which he can never progress. His perfectionist tendencies create a total block: he cannot proceed, because he wants to get things absolutely right, and he craves recognition not just for good-quality work but for an exceptional achievement. However, he succeeds in maintaining his self-motivation and self-discipline since writing provides some degree of meaning for the final days of his life.

A more famous example of writer's block is considered in a 2004 article by Joan Acocella where she describes the experiences of the poet Coleridge who wrote in 1832, 'Yesterday was my birthday. So completely has a whole year passed with scarcely the fruits of a month. O Sorrow and Shame … I have done nothing!'

To increase his levels of creativity, Coleridge took opium and experienced what he described as 'visions' while in a state of semi-consciousness. When he woke up completely, he would attempt to record his visions. On one occasion, the poet had been reading an account of the emperor Kublai Khan building a magnificent palace. This led to a vision which prompted several hundred lines of poetry. Unfortunately, when he was writing down the words of his poem, a man appeared and knocked on his door, distracting him. The vision was lost, the writer became blocked and 'the man from Porlock' became a famous minor character in literary history. The poem 'Kubla Khan' was never finished to Coleridge's satisfaction.

In her article, Acocella also considers other views of writer's block, including the belief that it is a condition that can be treated with Prozac or Ritalin and is related to manic depression. In this interpretation, it is considered to be a kind of psychological disorder. At the other extreme lies the idea that 'some writers become blocked simply because the concept exists, and invoking it is easier than writing'.

So what might writer's block mean for PhD thesis writers? There are three specific questions that will need to be addressed:

1. In which situations does writer's block occur?
2. What are its causes?
3. What kind of strategies or solutions can we use to overcome it?

▶ In which situations does writer's block occur?

Below are the thoughts of first- and second-year PhD students at two UK universities, compiled from group discussions which took place over a four-year period.

Box 11.1. Writer's block occurs when ...

a. I don't know how or where to begin.
b. I thought I knew what I wanted to write but suddenly I realize that I'm not so sure.
c. I lose the plot and can't remember what I want to say next.
d. I lose any sense of direction and don't know where my writing is leading me.
e. I feel that what I am writing is trivial and of no real interest to the reader.
f. I get distracted by other ideas which are on my mind.
g. I have so many ideas at once that I cannot get any of them down on paper.
h. I keep writing the same section/paragraph and cannot seem to go beyond it.
i. I lose interest in what I am writing.
j. What I am writing has stopped making sense to me.
k. Ideas start jumping around all over the place.

Evidently, some of these situations can be considered more serious than others. The students elaborated on some of the reasons given, as follows:

> It is frustrating not to be able to get all those ideas down. Some people can manage this orally, but not in writing. The problem is lack of focus perhaps. (statement g)
>
> This is the normal experience, I think. What causes that? It's possible that you shouldn't have started it or maybe you are being too perfectionist rather than moving on. There could be a lot of causes, but this to me is a fairly normal situation, something that we all experience. (h)
>
> Certain chapters block me, particularly results chapters. I can lose interest in certain chapters. (i)
>
> A chapter that I thought was really awful had to be left till the end. I came back to it and still wasn't very pleased with it. (e)
>
> Losing sense of the structure became a big issue for me at the very beginning. (a)

In such discussions, writers will make a clear distinction between becoming blocked at the very start of writing and the occurrence of a blockage which appears while writing. The former can present a significant obstacle for a minority of writers, who either lack the impetus to get started or feel over-whelmed by the enormity of the task ahead. Once a clear starting point has been established, the problem can disappear.

More commonly, you will find that you have little difficulty in getting started and that your initial motivation levels are high. First draft writing will, however, present situations in which you feel that you cannot proceed. If it is a case of having too many ideas (statements g and k) or losing the plot (c), this can be considered a normal occurrence and part of the writing process for which a number of solutions can be readily applied. Unfortunately, some of the situations mentioned above do not fall into this category and are considered below.

I feel that what I am writing is trivial and of no real interest to the reader

You may have such feelings about certain parts of your text – for example, a section of the literature review or the description of your data collection methods. In such a situation, you can say to yourself, 'This all seems rather obvious. However, I know that in the next section what I have to say is of interest and I have full confidence in it'. A lack of confidence in the entire text is a more serious matter.

When inexperienced researchers present their work to others, a common reaction is surprise that colleagues in the field are genuinely interested in what they have to say. Positive feedback can generate confidence and prevent writers from being drawn into the lack of self-belief which is a major cause of blockage. It therefore makes good sense to seek out opportunities for gaining feedback on your work through conference presentations, departmental seminars and discussion groups.

I lose interest in what I am writing

At a certain point, you may find yourself thinking, 'I feel I was once interested in this project, but I no longer am'. Deciding on a research topic in haste or gradually realizing that there is a lack of interest by others in your field may have caused this to happen. The result can be a complete change of direction or even the abandonment of the research topic. Sometimes, however, a project can be saved if you are able to identify some element that still interests you, as in the example below:

Box 11.2. One writer's experience

From the beginning of my research I found great difficulty in developing my own research questions ... but in the eighth month of my PhD my second supervisor started to help me. I went back to my reading and found a connection between what I really wanted to do and the suggestions that the second supervisor gave me. I realized that I was in charge of my PhD thesis and that I had to develop the research questions. I had thought it would be easier to answer someone else's questions, but I realized that I needed to be more independent. One of my problems had been that I had misunderstood 'independence' and thought that it meant doing everything on my own, whereas I needed a guide. And I confused 'guidance' with being told what to do ...

I have now changed my topic and my first supervisor. I found that when we met, he was always talking about his preferred topic and I wanted to talk about mine. But the topic has to be my responsibility. What helped me to go on was having the real research questions in my heart.

Researchers in certain science subject areas who apply to join an existing project may also experience doubts about ownership of their own research. They may wonder to themselves, 'Do I have anything significant to add to this project? Is it really my area of interest or that of my supervisor? Am I saying what my supervisor wants me to say rather than what I want to say?'

If you feel that you do not really have ownership rights of your PhD research project, or if you believe that you are merely repeating the work of someone else, then you can become blocked. You begin to feel that what you are doing is not worth continuing because other people have said it or others could say it better. Once you begin to experience these feelings, the next step may be to lose interest in your work. It is a situation that cannot be ignored.

What I am writing has stopped making sense to me

If ideas stop making sense in one or two paragraphs, there may be a problem of coherence that needs to be addressed. If, however, you feel that the whole text no longer makes sense, this is more serious. In the discussion of research topic feasibility (in Chapter 2), the particular problem of studying phenomena that are evolving was mentioned. In such cases, it can happen that you suddenly realize that the focus of your research has changed and that your previously stated aims are no longer valid or applicable. This, in turn, can lead to feeling that the whole project is worthless or senseless. Here is another writer's experience:

> When I submitted my draft to the supervisory board, they told me that it wasn't a draft – it was just a collection of notes. I had spent a lot of time on this. I really didn't know what to do until a supervisor encouraged me and gave some useful advice.

In conclusion, there are multiple situations in which writer's block can affect you, but some are clearly more serious than others, especially those in which you question the meaning or the ownership of what you are doing. Nelson's argument that being blocked can be a positive experience is valid only up to a point: some blockages not only stop you in your tracks but can prove to be terminal. A review of reasons for quitting a PhD published by the *Thesis Whisperer* website in 2014 (see Appendix 1) reveals that these tend to include the following:

- problems with motivation, including boredom, disenchantment and laziness
- injury or illness
- family commitments, including marriage breakdowns
- loneliness
- lack of university jobs/attraction of a job offer
- problems in choice of topic
- cross-disciplinary research issues

- failed lab work
- problems with 'writing up'
- supervision issues (including neglect, incompetence and personality clashes)

Problems related to self-motivation and those related to writing-up feature prominently on this list and similar lists compiled elsewhere.

▶ **What are the causes of writer's block?**

The same groups of first- and second-year PhD students also discussed possible causes of writer's block and produced the list below:

Box 11.3. When I experience writer's block, the main causes are usually ...

a. outside distractions
b. lack of time
c. tiredness
d. general anxiety
e. perfectionism
f. trying to live up to very high standards established by others
g. lack of confidence in the end product
h. thinking which is muddled or blinkered
i. a feeling that I am heading up a blind alley or running out of options
j. procrastination: putting off big decision-making
k. an inability to impose a clear structure on my writing
l. a premonition that I am heading for ultimate failure – so why bother?
m. not reading enough that is relevant to what I have to write
n. a lack of ideas or lack of knowledge
o. negative feedback from readers
p. language difficulties

Some suggestions (a, b) relate to the fact that we need to balance writing with the rest of our life. Further discussion of these specific points revealed a whole range of anxieties, even concerning seemingly trivial activities, such as finding time for cleaning an oven. 'Outside distractions' can also include major life events which cause you to stop writing. It seems that stopping very abruptly for such reasons without thinking about the stopping point can cause a greater blockage later on. When you eventually return to your writing, it is often harder to reconnect.

Perfectionism and general anxiety, which appear to be closely linked, are mentioned by many writers as catalysts for writer's block. An additional problem is that perfectionist tendencies and their negative consequences can go unrecognized in the early stages of writing. It appears entirely normal to want to do everything exceptionally well and to insist even in the beginning on the highest standards. Ultimately, this may prove to be an advantage when editing a final draft of a long text. For first draft writing we need to control our perfectionist tendencies or risk becoming blocked by the same section of text, or paragraph, or even sentence.

As was the case with typical situations, some of the perceived causes of writer's block require closer consideration, including the following:

Trying to live up to very high standards established by others

> For me, it is linked to the general PhD framework. Is the work that I am producing of a high enough standard? (1st-year PhD student)

This possible reason for writer's block seems to be closely associated with a 'lack of confidence in the end product'. Both are a serious cause for concern. It is worth asking yourself who the 'others' that you are attempting to emulate might be. Other PhD researchers? Other authors? Editors of journals? Academics in the field?

For many writers, the idea of following in the footsteps of other authors and maintaining their standards is a daunting task. This can also lead to another possible reason for a block, the feeling that you need to read much more in order to be able to write at the same standard.

> I sometimes get this feeling that what I am writing is very thin in content, because I haven't read enough. Then I may get blocked like this.

This type of feeling with respect to a particular chapter (or section of a chapter) is common to all writers. If the standards that you are aiming for are apparent in sections of your text, it is entirely logical to feel dissatisfied when other sections do not measure up. Such situations are manageable: it is often sufficient to make a careful note of the nature of the problem and then move on. A more general feeling that you are failing to meet the standards set by others is, however, more serious.

Language difficulties

Many PhD researchers who study in the UK are disadvantaged to some degree by the fact that English is not their native language. My own experience of attempting to learn nine foreign languages at various stages of my life makes me sympathetic to this situation. I believe that I can express ideas in my own language with a fair degree of fluency and coherence, which in turn gives me the confidence to believe that I can usually convey a message to a listener or reader without being misunderstood. On those occasions when I have been obliged to deliver a lecture or write a coherent academic text in a foreign language, I have found this to be a frustrating and demanding experience.

If this is your situation, you will realize that there are no instant solutions but that the sympathetic support of supervisors is crucial to your success. According to Paltridge and Starfield (2007: 43–4) a common cause of writer's block may be the fear of somehow being 'an impostor'. This can affect second-language writers more acutely than those writing in their first language if perceptions of intellectual ability and language proficiency are closely associated.

The same authors believe that perfectionism can be an added burden for the second-language writer. If every grammatical structure and all spelling need to be 100 per cent accurate, this will distract considerably from the more central task of producing a coherent first draft. Once the final draft has been reached, help is available through proofreading and copyediting services, which enable writers to submit their texts fully confident that language errors have been eliminated. For first draft writing, however, the struggle to express complex ideas when linguistic resources may be lacking can easily lead to a block.

> *The good thing in my department is that we don't have to write till the third year.* (1st-year PhD student)

Some supervisors and university departments respond to language problems by encouraging the postponement of writing until as late a stage as possible, arguing that by the third year, the standard of written English of the PhD researcher concerned will have improved. As has been made clear throughout this handbook, I do not support this approach. Instead of putting off writing in the early stages of research, it is advisable to begin developing effective writing skills as soon as possible. By the time that you reach the third year of PhD study, you will be more skilled and will feel more confident. This appears to be true not only for second-language writers but also for first-language writers, particularly those who have spent a considerable period of time away from the academic world.

In conclusion, it can be argued that there are no dominant causes of writer's block. A single writer may experience different types of blockages on different occasions and with different causes. However, it is evident that some of the causes will need more careful attention than others as the type of block that they produce may have serious consequences for the entire research project.

Interestingly, one participant in the discussions suggested that a major cause of being blocked might be fear of writer's block itself: in other words, the fear of becoming blocked might act as a self-fulfilling prophecy. It is very likely that regarding writer's block almost as a psychological or a medical condition in this way would be conducive to creating more anxiety rather than less.

▶ What kind of strategies or solutions can we use for writer's block?

Nelson (1993) believes that experiencing writer's block involves making a choice that you are not aware of. According to this view, the block does not appear of its own accord but is often there for a significant reason. The same author argues that 'trying to muscle our way past resistance doesn't work'. This is good advice. If the block is there for a reason, forcing a way through it is unlikely to succeed. Instead, blocked writers will find that there are a range of practical solutions available to them. The nature of the blockage will determine which is most likely to succeed.

One well-meant piece of advice often given to blocked writers is to switch to a different activity or to take a break from writing. Sometimes, this straightforward advice may work, but on other occasions it may actually make the situation worse. If you cannot write on Monday for some reason, going away for a few days' holiday or changing activities can leave you feeling refreshed. However, there is no reason to believe that this will result in an effortless reconnection with your text on Friday or Saturday. The blockage will most probably still be there and may even appear to be worse.

In fact, one major cause of writer's block to be added to those detailed in the previous section can be an *inability to reconnect with previous thinking*. You look at (for example) a draft of Chapter 2 that was produced several weeks ago and cannot discover a thread of argumentation that links this text to other texts. It is almost a case of wondering, 'Did I really write this?' or 'What was I thinking at the time?' As noted in Chapter 3, a similar break-down can occur when attempting to reconnect to reading texts when the content has been half-forgotten. So, the advice to go away and get some fresh air can be helpful up to a point, especially in cases where this is only for a few minutes. However, if you go away for a week and come back, you may find that you are even more blocked than you were before. Worst of all, you may not be able to remember the circumstances in which the blockage took place.

To prevent such situations from occurring, it is useful to consider how you record your ideas as they occur. Analytic notes (see Chapter 3) are the starting point: these can be developed into the kind of memos described by Hammersley and Atkinson (1983). Alternatively, they can be integrated into an ongoing reflective journal of the kind mentioned in Chapter 10, with these added advantages:

- It can become an important document in its own right, recording why you made certain decisions at certain stages.
- By mediating between the writer and the text, it can help to create intellectual distance as part of a more reasoned and objective analysis.

A reflective journal can also contribute to the monitoring of progress and encourage critical self-appraisal, as was discussed in Chapter 10. If it works well, it can document the intellectual journey that will result in the final version of the written text. At the same time, it can provide a source of encouragement and self-motivation, especially if it is shared with other writers.

It seems that talking to yourself and writing notes to yourself are useful strategies both to prevent and to manage writer's block and its consequences. Sometimes a problem that seems severe one week will have diminished the next. Perhaps in a different part of your work, you will discover ideas that can help address problems that are apparently insoluble. There are also occasions when problem areas can appear to get worse. In either case, you need to try to rationalize and to record events as you see them.

Rationalizing events means conducting a dialogue with yourself – one that will help you achieve a distance between yourself and the text that you are attempting to produce. The most important step is to write to yourself at the point of blockage before you walk away. You may say to yourself, 'At this moment, I am stuck. I think the reason is X…I am therefore leaving this chapter but will come back later.' This kind of record will provide you with a significant amount of help when you return to the text and wish to reconnect. If, at the point of return, you cannot remember the circumstances in which you stopped writing, the blockage is more likely to continue and perhaps increase.

Other writers offer a range of practical suggestions that will help combat first draft blockages. Zerubavel (1999) recommends a change in the type of writing that you are engaged in. If you reach an apparent dead end, switch to a less demanding type of writing, such as transcribing data, and come back later. Dunleavy (2003: 138) recommends regular use of the printer for sections of text that appear to resist completion on the grounds that spreading out pages of written text rather than staring at a screen can sometimes provide you with the broader perspective that you may need. Murray (2002), emulating Steinbeck, recommends free writing for five minutes or longer. The aim is to increase both fluency and confidence in writing. When a blockage does occur or a dead end is reached, writing can still continue.

The idea that writing can be a release from writing is an interesting suggestion. If you cannot continue with one type of writing, try another. If you keep writing in some other way, you are still writing. If you are blocked in one way, you can unblock in another. Sometimes this may even help you with the problem that caused the original blockage.

The list of strategies suggested by our groups of PhD researchers was as follows:

Box 11.4. Writer's block strategies and solutions

a. I tell myself to persevere and that determination will win out.
b. I walk away and do something completely different.
c. I skip what I am writing and try another writing task.
d. I change the location of where I write.
e. I change the time of day when I write.
f. I play some soothing music.
g. I offer myself some kind of reward or incentive.
h. I talk to someone about the blockage.
i. I talk to myself about the blockage.
j. I print out a section of my work and examine it off-screen.
k. I try to get inspiration from reading something relevant.
l. I write to myself before I walk away.

The solutions or strategies that will best suit your own circumstances cannot easily be predetermined, although a safe prediction can be made that perseverance alone (strategy *a*) is unlikely to succeed. Strategies *b–g* offer a range of practical solutions, any of which may be of some help. Strategies *h–l* are perhaps the most likely to be effective on a consistent basis, for reasons which were discussed earlier in this chapter section.

Perhaps, the most useful general advice is to try to become more aware of how you approach writing and the small steps that you can take that can make a real difference in achieving success. An interesting awareness-raising experience is to be shadowed in your daily activities. This happened to me at a university where I once worked as a head of department and where as part of a research project I was accompanied by a Master's level management student. This person followed me everywhere I went during my working hours, noting down everything that I did and drawing conclusions on how I spent my time. The findings were predictable: it seemed that I was wasting many hours of the day on seemingly unimportant tasks, most of which involved the telephone (as these events took place in the pre-digital age).

This was the first time I had really thought about my professional activities in a measured way. The obvious conclusion appeared to be that I could become much more efficient and could allocate more time to a larger number of activities, thus achieving more. However, the more I reflected on this, the more I realized that the time that I was apparently wasting was actually of great importance. In a stressful job, I was giving myself as much breathing space as I could and therefore allowing myself time to think.

Similarly, one possible solution for writer's block is to give yourself the time, space and distance that you need. Rather than forcing yourself to write, taking a break at exactly the right time can actually help. This is not because distracting yourself is necessarily a solution but because your brain does need to recover from the tiredness caused by the demands of first draft writing. If you are engaged in an activity that requires your complete attention, then from time to time you will need to provide some space to allow new creative ideas to come in – including solutions to problems that may appear to be virtually insoluble. At the same time, allowing some distance to emerge between yourself and the sources of a block may provide you with the opportunity to develop a new perspective on what you have written.

▶ Coping with rejection

Self-motivation for writing needs to be nurtured not only during the years of PhD study but also as part of a career in academia. Submitting early drafts of texts to a PhD supervisor may be the first occasion (but it will not be the last) when your written work is subjected to rigorous criticism and possible rejection. The first time that you submit an article to a respected journal only to see it rejected can constitute a major blow to both your self-confidence and your ability to motivate yourself for further writing. Similarly, when a chapter submitted to a PhD supervisor receives negative feedback, this can be an important event in your development as a research writer.

The first reaction to rejection is usually a mix of shock and anger. Most reputable academic journals will provide feedback that is both useful and informative if you consider it carefully. Some of the criticism will be justified, some perhaps not. First, you must recover from the psychological blow of realizing that your efforts have been considered inadequate by specialists in your field. In a normal series of events, you will then absorb the feedback, pick yourself up and overcome your disappointment. This process is likely to repeat itself throughout your career until you establish a reputation as an accomplished writer within your disciplinary area.

When supervisors give feedback, they also have a duty to provide comments that are useful and informative (see Chapter 7). They may also be well equipped to advise you on how to turn rejection into renewed self-motivation. One strategy is to ask them directly what they did the first time they had examples of their own writing rejected. Each will have a story to tell and words of advice to pass on. The following example is taken from a series of interviews with academics who have already established their reputation as writers within various fields.

Box 11.5. A PhD supervisor's perspective

This has happened to everyone at some point. The more you apply, the more you will be rejected but also the greater the chance that something will be accepted. You have to remind yourself that this also happens to professors who have been in the field for a long time. It also sometimes has to do with sending something to the wrong kind of journal. There may also be a subjective element in the peer-review process. The important thing is not to take rejection personally. Always take it as an opportunity to reflect on what could have been done better. Share the feedback with someone else and then persevere. It's part of the game. (Professor of gender studies)

Looking from a publisher perspective is also useful when coping with rejection of articles submitted to journals. Publishers may have very large numbers of articles to process and to choose from. Your article may be of good quality, but a similar contribution may already have been accepted. We assume that rejection means that our work is inadequate, but this assumption may well be wrong. The only certainty is that being rejected is part of life in academia. It is an experience that every research writer will go through in an increasingly competitive environment.

Action Points

1. During first draft writing, ensure that <u>sufficient time and space is provided for self-monitoring</u>. An important element within this process is to make yourself fully aware of the importance of the affective aspects of writing.
2. At every stage of writing, <u>examine your expectations</u> to make sure that they are realistic.
3. Find suitable ways of <u>managing stress and overcoming perfectionist</u> tendencies. There are a range of solutions from which you can choose.
4. Consider a <u>writing journal</u> as a means of keeping track of your progress and maintaining self-motivation.
5. <u>Respond thoughtfully</u> to both positive and negative feedback. Be willing to learn from mistakes and put them behind you.

12 Reporting and Analysing Research Findings

This chapter

- considers different approaches to reporting and analysing PhD research data as part of first draft writing
- discusses ways in which you can highlight and draw conclusions from your key findings

▶ Structuring your data report

The expectation of many readers is that the data report section of the PhD thesis will define your work and highlight its originality and even its uniqueness. Such readers may be impressed by the depth of analysis within your literature review or the quality of your research design, but arguably, what will interest them most will be the research findings themselves and your interpretation and analysis of what you have found.

Some writers consider this to be the most complex and demanding element of the PhD thesis, while others such as Dornyei (2007: 280) believe that it is relatively straightforward because there are well-established formats to guide writers. However, while there may be agreed formats in certain disciplinary areas, difficult choices may need to be made in others. There are a number of potential danger areas to consider:

- The quantity of data collected may cause some writers to feel that they are blocked at the very beginning of the reporting exercise.
- The report and accompanying analysis may fail to do justice to the quality of the data collected.

- If key findings are not clearly highlighted, the reader may become lost amidst all of the detail.
- It may be difficult to achieve a clear structure for the narrative element and coherence for both narrative and analysis.

To provide a clear structure for the data report, there is sometimes an assumption that a PhD thesis should contain a 'results' chapter, as is often the case at Master's level. Brewer (2007: 144) talks in these terms when he says:

> The results chapter needs to present clearly the findings that you have established. This is more difficult than it may sound, and prior planning of the chapter and in particular the order in which results are to be presented is necessary.

The idea of a 'results chapter' may be appropriate in some cases but seems over-simplistic for many research projects at PhD level. However, this author is justified in pointing out that structuring such a chapter (or chapters) will require a careful consideration of all of the available options. An added difficulty is that you will also need to decide how to balance the reporting of what you have found with your analysis of the findings. Will you tell a story without interruption and then go on to analyse the events that take place? Will your analysis be built into the narrative as it progresses? How can this be achieved while maintaining the coherence of your narrative?

Deciding how to conduct data reporting and analysis can have significant consequences and can radically alter the final PhD thesis. It is therefore worth considering first of all how your data reporting might be structured. Here are some of the more common alternatives.

According to your data collection methods

This is a very simple way of organizing and displaying research findings. For example, data from questionnaires is reported, followed by interview data and finally observation notes. The main drawback of this type of approach is that your analysis will need to link findings from different data sources as part of a triangulation process. Giving an account of the data from each source separately is unlikely to provide a sufficient basis for analysis. In addition, text organized along these lines will tend be predictable and even dull.

Quantitative data followed by qualitative data

This approach has similar drawbacks to the one described above. However, reporting on quantitative data followed by qualitative within each section of a chapter is a possibility. The analysis could then be conducted section by section, drawing together the different data sources. One PhD writer comments, 'This is possible if the reader needs one or the other first. An example would be where interviewees are chosen on the basis of quantitative data from questionnaires. But in many arts and humanities subjects, it would still be abnormal and not taken seriously'.

Based on research questions or hypotheses

Organization according to research questions or hypotheses is common practice in many disciplines, with sections of chapters focusing on each individual research question or each numbered hypothesis. For those who consider research questions which are articulated at the beginning to be the fundamental building blocks of the research, this would be a suitable way to proceed. However, this is sometimes considered to be a rather unimaginative option, especially in cases where different research questions produce results of varying quality.

According to designated qualitative data analysis categories: key themes applied to the data or emerging from the data itself

Organization according to data analysis categories is popular (and sometimes mandatory) in many disciplines that encourage qualitative research. These data categories can be predetermined and imposed on the data, or they can be more fluid, emerging from the data as it is collected. The latter approach is associated with the type of ethnographic studies conducted in disciplines such as anthropology or sociology.

Whichever structure you choose will depend on a number of variables:

- the requirements of the disciplinary area(s) associated with the research
- the type of research questions and hypotheses that you have formulated
- the different types of data that you have collected
- your preferred reporting style
- the way in which you intend to integrate analysis into the report

The last point is one of the most important choices that you will be required to make. Your tasks are to report the findings clearly and coherently, to add your own analysis and to draw conclusions. There are two basic options for achieving this:

1. Report your data (tell the story) and then analyse later. ('Here is what I have found. Now let us consider what it all means....').
    Intuitively, this may seem the more logical and more straightforward choice. However, building a long narrative can be more complex than

it first appears. In the analysis, a partial retelling of the narrative may also be required so that links between the two are clearly established. The result can be that you are led into unintentionally repeating yourself many times.

2. Report the data and weave the analysis into the narrative. The story is told section by section, and you analyse as you go along. ('The first finding was … This seems to indicate that….').

    Weaving analysis into the tapestry of a narrative can be the most complex task in first draft writing but (arguably) one of the most rewarding. Each discussion of analytical points will cause you to digress from the story that you are reporting. The reader will require clear guidance in this process so as not to lose the thread of both narrative and accompanying analysis.

In fact, certain disciplinary areas may not allow a choice in this matter. Cargill and O'Connor (2012: 33) claim that certain science disciplines may issue guidelines advising that the 'results' and 'discussion' of experiments be presented separately, while others may allow a blending of narrative and analysis. Rules of engagement can be strict:

> If the separate style is used, it is generally important to confine any comments in the Results section to saying what the numbers show, without comparing them with other research or suggesting explanations.

At the other extreme, disciplines that promote data collection through ethnographic studies will generally proscribe the separation of data reporting and analysis. Emerson, Fretz and Shaw (1995) note that ethnographers are generally advised to develop a 'thematic narrative' when reporting their data:

> Writing a thematic narrative differs fundamentally from writing an analytic argument, both in the process of putting that text together and in the structure of the final text. Structurally, in a text which presents a logical argument, the author sets forth a formal thesis or proposition in the introduction as a stance to be argued, then develops each analytic point with evidence logically following from and supporting the propositional thesis. In contrast, an ethnographic story proceeds through an intellectual examination of evidence to eventually reach its contributing central idea.

You will need to discover the kind of logic that your readers will expect when reporting findings as part of first draft writing. Some questions to ask yourself can include the following:

- Will I be expected to report my results and analyse them as I present them?

- Will I be expected to provide a selection of key findings, a summary of all the findings or both?
- What kind of structure will be expected for the reporting of my data?
- Will I be required to use certain fixed formats for displaying data?
- If an interesting finding emerges, will it be appropriate to compare it with the findings of other researchers?
- When drawing conclusions, will I be expected to refer back to the literature as well as to my results?

▶ Reporting quantitative data

The aim of this section is to consider ways in which different types of quantitative data can be displayed and integrated into a text in order to report research findings. The emphasis here is on applying principles of clarity, conciseness and coherence rather than on considering in detail the merits and demerits of using tables, charts or other display formats. For this type of discussion, see, for example, Booth, Colomb and Williams (1995), Dunleavy (2003) or Dornyei (2007).

The guidelines that follow may not be needed by research writers in arts and humanities disciplines, where there is often a strong emphasis on qualitative research. They are also not intended as a detailed guide to report writing in science or social science disciplines: they do not, for example, provide advice that will help writers conduct the kind of statistical reasoning that forms the basis of the analysis of research findings in many areas. Useful help of this type is available elsewhere and is most unlikely to be generic: it is perhaps best provided from a range of disciplinary perspectives by authors such as Bruce, Pope and Stanistreet (2008) for health sciences, Howitt and Cramer (2003) for psychology or Seale (2004) for social sciences. Instead, we will consider how a 'clear presentation' of data can be best achieved. You will need to take into account the following steps:

1. *Make an informed decision concerning what to include and what to exclude.* It is unlikely that all of the data that has been collected can be included within your data report. Your selection decisions will depend on your research aims and the nature of the findings: you will normally include information that is <u>new, surprising or of clear significance to readers</u> in your field while excluding, summarizing or glossing over data which does not appear to fit these criteria.
2. *Highlight 'key findings' in context.* The more important the information that you wish to include, the more prominently it will need to be displayed. However, at this stage the context (other variables, other data

sets, for example) will also be needed; therefore, such findings cannot be presented in isolation. Your task will be to ensure that the most important information stands out so that it can be carefully analysed.

3. *Make the right choice of data display format.* The way you present your data is a question of choice. Here are some general points to consider:
   - Use *tables* rather than charts for large amounts of statistical data where great detail is required.
   - Use *charts* rather than tables to summarize and highlight certain aspects of the data, especially the comparison of key variables.
   - Pay careful attention to the labelling of both charts and tables to avoid ambiguity.
   - Consider using other 'nonstandard' formats such as maps or diagrams if they will help you to highlight important aspects of your data. Maps, for example, can be highly effective in showing the geographical spread of responses in a simple and straightforward way.

4. *To enable your readers to gain a perspective on what the data really means, plan a logical series of breakdowns.* Start with a more general or overall breakdown as in the example below based on data received from English language teachers where the scaled answers (0.00 – 3.50) refer to perceived frequency of use of technological devices:

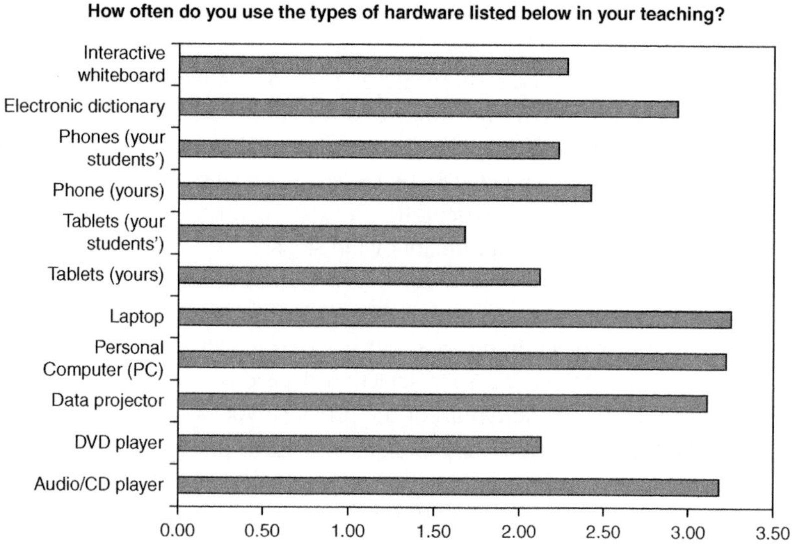

Fig 12.1 Use of technology in the English language classroom: an overview

Having provided an overall picture of technology use in the classroom, you can now proceed to more detailed breakdowns. You could, for example, explore the reasons for using particular technological devices related to the type of teaching or learning activity; you could present data that compare the use of mobile and non-mobile technology; you could divide the use of technology by teachers or students into three separate areas (during class time, as part of lesson preparation time, as an integral part of follow-up activities set as homework); you could focus on attitudes towards particular technological devices within each of these distinct areas.

For each separate breakdown, you will need to answer the following questions based on a checklist originally suggested by Denscombe (1998):

- What is my aim in displaying this particular data set?
- Is the choice of table, chart or other format appropriate?
- Have my tables, charts and other display formats been thoughtfully designed?
- Are tables and charts clearly labelled?
- Is there a danger of information overload?
- What further breakdowns might be required?

5. *Remember that the management of reader expectations is never more important than in chapters where you report your own data.* If you report on another person's research, readers will have the option of checking the reference to make sure that they have understood. With your findings, there is a need to be absolutely clear since there is no other source. If you have high-quality data, you cannot do justice to it if it becomes unclear as a result of your reporting.

After the data that you have selected has been clearly and carefully displayed, analysis may begin based on the narrative revealed by the numbers that you have presented. The ways in which you interpret your results may vary according to your disciplinary area, but the underlying aim of transforming data into 'new knowledge' remains the same.

▶ Reporting qualitative data

According to Miles and Huberman (1994) qualitative data is suited to 'locating meanings that people place on the events, processes and structures of their lives'. The focus is on naturally-occurring phenomena and natural settings, while there is an emphasis on richness, depth, and complexity. When writing up qualitative data, it is not as easy to prescribe choices in the way that Dunleavy, Dornyei and other writers suggest for quantitative data. Because qualitative data tends to be richer and more detailed, it is often more difficult to decide:

1. How much data should be reported? How much should be included in the text of 'reporting chapters' and how much added in appendices?
2. Which display formats are most suitable? Can qualitative data be reduced or summarized without changing its nature? How can you balance within these formats your own voice and those of participants in your research?

How much data should be reported?

It is not uncommon for writers to feel overwhelmed by the quantity of qualitative data collected and the task of reporting and analysing such data. How you do justice to this data and to the informants who have provided it is also a major concern. As a result, you may find it difficult to begin the reporting process unless you have a clear plan for data selection and reduction. According to Dey (1993: 242):

> Research is essentially an exercise in selection. If we still harbour any lingering illusions on this point, the discipline of producing an account of our analysis should dispel them.

This author recommends producing a tree-shaped diagram to represent the main and subsidiary themes of the research and the relevant data in each area. Decisions can then be made concerning which branches should be pruned and which should be allowed to flourish.

Many writers publish complete transcripts of raw qualitative data in the appendices section of their research. Even if some of this data has not been reported and analysed in detail, such transcripts may be of interest to many readers. The value of your original transcripts should not be underestimated.

Which display formats are most suitable?
Single quotations

The actual words that people use to express their views can be a more powerful source of evidence within a narrative than a reported, paraphrased or summarized version. Booth, Colomb and Williams (1995: 207) suggest that paraphrasing sources should be reserved for cases 'when you are more interested in findings and data than in how a source expresses them'. Actual quotations, on the other hand, give stronger emphasis to the speaker and their voice, meaning that research participants can achieve a degree of empowerment by gaining a presence within the report of your findings. Their voice will have been heard by others. One word of warning, however, comes from Holliday (2002), who argues that in some cases verbatim data can also 'serve to reduce, rather than enhance, the humanity of the participant' depending on the way in which it is reported within your text. Your task is to ensure that quotations do not in any way misrepresent the views of speakers or writers.

Multiple quotations

Qualitative research that depends heavily on multiple block quotations presents a problem for the writer. How can such evidence be displayed within the text without interrupting the flow of narration and analysis? Tables of quotations can provide a straightforward answer, presenting text rather than statistical data. In the following example, English language teachers are being interviewed to elicit attitudes to a new coursebook (Q3). Answers to this question can easily be compared using this format, with any interesting points of contrast or comparison highlighted. Responses to other questions (Q4, Q5) could also be added to this table to extend the display and its ability to allow certain themes to emerge for analysis:

Table 12.1 Multiple block quotations from a data report

Interviewee	*Q3. Overall effectiveness of the coursebook*
Teacher 1	The coursebook more or less covers all areas. Writing activities are the most interesting, reading is quite limited and texts are easy. Some nice speaking activities but I often link activities together or supplement them to adapt them to my students' needs.
Teacher 2	The book is not good enough for me. It's really messy, chaotic. There is a good deal of stuff inside the book, but it's not easy for the student to make sense of it, because it is not presented in an organized way.
Teacher 3	Listening, speaking, reading and writing are equally and successfully distributed in the coursebook. Pronunciation is not covered, but it's not that necessary, because it's quite advanced for this level.
Teacher 4	All of the coursebook skills are poor. The texts (listening and reading) are poor, and they don't offer opportunities for follow-up questions, discussion, speaking.
Teacher 5	The coursebook has limited grammar. I would like to have more exercises. The speaking activities are not bad, but beginner level students find them difficult.

Case studies

According to Grbich (2007), case studies can be presented in different 'subformats'. They might consist of narratives delivered by participants in their own words, summaries of participant testimony provided by an author or a mix of the two. Yin (1994) identifies four distinct reporting varieties, ranging from straightforward single descriptive narratives to complex multiple narratives. Whichever approach you choose, you will be producing some kind of illustrative account of events highlighting specific issues that are relevant to your research. Case studies are widely used for reporting research data in areas such as law, medicine, public administration and management.

Vignettes

A vignette is a slightly different type of illustrative story, often used to clarify a particular point or perspective regarding some finding in the data. The stories are presented in an indirect manner as in the fabricated example below:

Box 12.1. A sample vignette

Y, a 93 year old British woman of Irish descent, was referred to a neuropsychologist for assessment by the Thames stroke unit following an ischaemic attack. She reported left-sided weakness, feeling disorientated and frequently fatigued. She is widowed and lives alone but has family members visiting regularly and assisting with care. The neuropsychologist assessed her verbal memory, visual memory, processing speed and cognitive abilities and found a significant decline across most modalities, which is consistent with her son's observations of her changes. He noticed that her short term memory has declined whilst her long term memory functioning was relatively intact. She was able to recount specific autobiographical memories in vivid detail of her role in the Second World War, yet unable to recall recently asked information. During the assessment, when asked background information, she discussed a specific date 60 years ago, including what she ate, the colour of her uniform and the names of all her colleagues in her regiment. Results also indicated that Y has several strengths, such as her visual-processing abilities and abstract reasoning. A specific rehabilitation plan should be implemented (commencing next week) with assisted physical care when her family is not able to visit, in order to recover from the effects of her recent stroke and challenges.

In a research context vignettes allow you to report the experiences of vulnerable participants in an indirect way with minimal possibility of identifying the people concerned. They are commonly used in psychology and different branches of medicine, but I have also seen them used effectively in social science areas such as religious studies, describing, for example, cases of apostasy where the research participants might be in danger if their identities were revealed.

Layers

The data that you have collected may also be displayed in layers, defined as 'the interweaving of different voices to juxtapose their views, for example sequential narratives on how an accident happened or how a marriage was broken.' (Grbich 2007). A layered data display is useful when different perspectives need to be included within a single report. A more complex version of this is known as a *pastiche*, in which fragments of data representing different views of participants may be juxtaposed. For more information about both types of display, see Frost (2011).

There are many excellent sources of further guidance in the reporting and subsequent analysis of qualitative data. Dey (1993), Hammersley and Atkinson (1983), Miles and Huberman (1994) and Cresswell (2003) all provide in-depth discussions that can build on the ideas presented briefly in this section.

▶ Drawing conclusions

Whether you are reporting quantitative data, qualitative data or a mix of the two, the way in which you present the conclusions drawn from your key findings will define your work and may determine its degree of success. In this final section, we present some practical guidelines to help you achieve this. See also the comments in Chapter 6, Section 2, on writing 'Conclusions' chapters.

Clearly highlight your key findings

As indicated in the previous sections of this chapter, the first important step in providing meaningful analysis is to isolate and highlight key findings. These could be categorized as those which appear to be:

- the most relevant in terms of research questions and hypotheses
- the most interesting, allowing new ideas and theories to emerge
- the most convincing, building on ideas from previous research

- the most surprising, contradicting your own assumptions and those of other writers or producing different results from previous research

Explain the significance of the findings to researchers in your field

All of the above elements may contribute to the perceived significance of your research findings. The next step is to prioritize, explaining which findings appear to be most significant for readers in your field or related fields. An example is given below from my own research into post-1989 changes in the education system in Slovakia:

Box 12.2. Teachers' changing perceptions of students, students' parents and themselves

Another type of change which Slovak teachers are having to adjust to concerns their own roles as teachers, and their relationship with students and the parents of students. The evidence from the case study data shows that teachers are finding it difficult to come to terms with what they feel is a reduced status for themselves in the post-1989 educational world. The tradition of the 'teacher-scholar' (see previous section) seems long gone, and teachers feel less appreciated, especially by parents (see, for example, comments by A. p.157). A highly experienced gymnazium teacher, M. (p.173 & 169) believes that in the new Slovakia people are generally more business-oriented and respect businessmen more and the teaching profession less, while children emulate their parents' diminishing respect by being less well-behaved in class. In all of the focus group interviews there were some participants who lamented the general decline in student behaviour, which they explain in one of two ways: either students are less passive and more ready to question the teacher's authority (M., p.161), or students have been influenced by the lack of stimulus at home and the fact that education is not valued as much as it was (S., p.161).

In the new post-1989 Slovakia some students now have opportunities to travel to English-speaking countries which were denied to their parents. In the opinion of G., (p.174), this puts extra pressure on teachers of English, since such students are likely to return speaking English which they judge to be more fluent than that of their teachers. While teachers believe that in terms of language knowledge and accuracy they are still well ahead of even those students who travel abroad (see A's comments, p.178), nevertheless they realize that returnees can seriously disrupt the way in which they teach their classes and thus threaten their authority. (Thomas 1999)

In this particular case, the change in perception of teacher status was a major finding. The significance of this finding was emphasized in two ways:

- by referring back to the literature on the 'teacher-scholar' and the assumptions made by writers, which appeared to be out of date
- by referring to sources within the data itself to corroborate the finding

The analysis could then continue by examining the implications of these apparent threats to the authority of teachers in a changing educational environment.

Critically reflect on the research process itself

For most writers this consists of pointing out one or two limitations in the study or gaps that need to be filled by other researchers – a standard convention within 'Conclusion' sections of PhD theses. However, it is possible and fruitful to take this process a little further. The end point of your data collection and analysis provides an excellent opportunity to reflect on the whole process of research design, planning of data collection, implementation of data collection, data analysis and even the process of writing up the data. The following are the kind of questions you could ask yourself and attempt to answer:

- What aspects of the research design appear to have been the most and least successful?
- How satisfied am I with the quality of the data that was collected?
- What choices did I make in planning and implementing data collection? In retrospect, would I make any different decisions?
- How successful have I been in linking the findings of my research to the concerns of readers in my field (or related fields)?
- If I were to replicate this research with the same focus and questions, what would I do differently?

Action Points

1. Before determining the structure and approach of your data report, consider the expectations of important readers, such as your supervisor(s). The decisions that you make will have a significant effect on how you communicate your findings.
2. Ensure that your data is clearly displayed either within the text or in appendices before you begin to conduct your analysis. Key decisions

concern what to include or exclude and how you will highlight main findings through well-chosen display formats.

3. Display data <u>in sequential steps</u>, beginning with an overall view and gradually narrowing down to specific details.

4. Pay careful attention to the <u>labelling</u> of any charts, tables or diagrams so that you avoid ambiguity.

5. Highlight the <u>most relevant, most interesting, most convincing and most surprising findings</u> when you read through your data and when you report it in writing.

6. Critically reflect on the whole <u>process of identifying and writing up key findings</u>: these reflections can form an important part of the final chapter of your thesis.

13 Completing your PhD Thesis

> *This chapter*
>
> - *outlines the final stages of PhD thesis writing*
> - *explores the editing process and provides a series of practical checklists to help you edit different aspects of your work*
> - *examines the role of oral presentations both as a means of clarifying your thinking and as preparation for the viva*

▶ Writing the final version

Once the first draft has been completed and major revisions such as the reordering, division or exclusion of chapters have taken place, a new phase in writing can begin. This <u>editing stage</u> may still involve making substantial changes that will affect chapter content, such as:

- seeing whether the same or similar ideas are unintentionally repeated in different parts of the text and taking appropriate action
- looking for unexplained contradictions in different parts of the text and deciding whether you need to justify or remove them
- cutting entire paragraphs or chapter sections that seem to create unnecessary digressions from your main arguments

At the other extreme, there will be more detailed changes that need to be made in your text. These are the types of changes that Murray (2002) refers to when she draws a distinction between editing and 'polishing' a text:

> *This is the time for revisions so fine that they do not seem worth making. It all begins to seem a bit pedantic, with more attention to the correctness of grammar and punctuation than to the research and your contribution. This is as it should be.*

Understanding the differences between the different types of editing is a necessary part of the writing process. Arguably, 'polishing' or proofreading a text should come at the very end, once other aspects of editing have been completed. Before this final stage, it is advisable to work through a series of other checklists that you can use as clear points of reference when you re-read your first draft.

Editing checklists are a useful tool as part of the process of monitoring progress in writing: when you are aiming to improve your writing through editing, you will need to break this process down, as there are so many different aspects of writing that can be problematic. Some will be easier to address than others. You will find it helpful to refer to three distinct kinds of lists, each of which will be examined in turn, relating to *text content*, *structure*, *coherence*, *clarity* and *style*. Finally, a separate list will be needed to help you check the *punctuation*, *spelling*, *grammar* and *layout* of each chapter in turn.

Content checklists

Content-editing lists serve two distinct purposes. First, they can remind you of all of the different elements that will need to be included in a standard PhD thesis and how they can be made to relate to each other effectively. Note that for 'Creative', 'by papers' PhDs or professional doctorates, an adapted list of items will be required. Second, they can help you check for more general content-related issues, such as missing or superfluous information in your text.

Table 13.1 Content checklist A

	Included? Finalized?	Your comments
Thesis title		
Abstract		
Acknowledgements		
Table of contents		
List of figures/maps/charts/diagrams		
Glossary of key terms/abbreviations or symbols used		
Statement of research aims		
Statement of research questions		
Context/background/reasons for the research		
Principal claims or hypotheses and their significance		

Theoretical frameworks for the research		
Exploration of key concepts		
Literature review		
Description of research methodology and data collection methods		
Reporting and analysis of data		
Summary of key findings		
Conclusions from the findings, their implications and significance		
Bibliography and references		
Appendices		

All (or some) of the boxes in this list may need to be ticked. Have all relevant items been included? Have they been finalized or do they require further attention? Among these items, you may need to pay particular attention to checking the following:

Your abstract: The abstract is an important document that needs to be well crafted and polished 'like a sign outside a shop inviting customers to come in', according to one PhD student. In particular, you will need to confirm that the content of the abstract and that of the introductory chapter match each other without any apparent inconsistencies.

Your research questions: These may need to be revisited even at this late stage. Can they be expressed more clearly to eliminate any form of ambiguity? The same check should be applied to any hypotheses or claims. Do any questions or claims need to be omitted?

Your literature review: There are many important points to confirm here:

- Is it clear what you are trying to achieve through your review?
- Do review sections do more than just report what others have to say about the underlying themes of your research?
- Have you clearly highlighted inconsistencies, things that other writers have missed or apparent contradictions in previous research findings?
- Are there any key authors or references missing that should be included?

Your data reporting and data analysis: This is another section of the thesis where a number of checks need to be applied:

- Have you reported all the important findings emerging from your data?
- Have you achieved an appropriate balance between different perspectives emerging from the data?
- Have links been established between your findings and previous research documented in the literature?
- Is there a suitable balance between data included within the text, data displayed in appendices and data that has not been reported?
- Have the identities of participants been anonymized when this is required?

Your conclusions section: This needs to demonstrate the *significance of the study and the contribution that it is making to your field of expertise.* Check that all of the different strands of the research have been pulled together. If there any loose ends, these should be made explicit wherever possible.

In addition to these items relating to specific sections of your text, there are also more general content-related issues that will need to be considered across all chapters. In each case, you will need to decide on the specific actions that are required. For example, in the first box of Table 13.2 below, 'duplication of content in different chapters or sections' might be addressed simply by cross-referencing in cases where the duplication is intentional or necessary. On the other hand, in situations that involve unintentional duplication you might decide to move pieces of text from one chapter to another or to omit certain paragraphs altogether. It is worth bearing in mind that, initially, you might decide to do none of these but simply note the duplication for future reference.

Table 13.2 Content checklist B

Editing task	Comments and actions
Check for <u>duplication of content</u> in different chapters or sections of the text	*Move sections of text? Which? Where? Omit sections of text? Which? Cross-reference content?*
Look for <u>apparent contradictions</u> in different parts of the text	
<u>Clarify any explanations</u> that may seem unclear	
Add or cut <u>illustrative examples</u>	
<u>Transfer content</u> to tables, footnotes or appendices	

<u>Balance content</u> between different chapters or chapter sections	
<u>Add words, phrases or sentences</u> where you feel arguments have been diluted in some way	
Reduce or increase the number of <u>quotations and references</u> within the text	
<u>Cut out any words, phrases or sentences</u> that seem unnecessary	

The basic actions for editing for content can be summarized for convenience:

- *omitting* text content
- *reducing* text content
- *adding* extra arguments or information
- *reordering* ideas within a text
- *summarizing* ideas within a text
- *changing* the words, expressions or sentences in some way
- *clarifying* the words, expressions or sentences in some way
- *highlighting* important information or arguments
- *combining* ideas within a text
- *comparing and contrasting* ideas within a text
- *transferring or moving* text content

Any of these may play an important part in the editing process. Although most of the content will already be in place, your first draft will gain a sharper focus and an increased level of coherence once actions such as these have been performed.

Structure checklist
This list will enable you to check the organizational breakdown of the thesis and the degree to which clear labelling helps with the effective management of reader expectations:

Table 13.3 Structure checklist

	Checked? Finalized?	*Your comments*
Informative, inclusive <u>thesis title</u>		
<u>Clear labelling</u> of chapters and chapter sections		
Carefully drafted <u>introductions</u>		
Interim and end-of-chapter <u>conclusions</u>		
<u>Signposting</u> within the text: forward and backward referencing		

→

Clear and consistent <u>paragraphing</u> within the text		
Avoidance of <u>over-organization</u> and <u>under-organization</u>		

Although structural checks are largely self-explanatory, it is worth highlighting the following points. See Chapter 6 for further discussion of each.

Chapter labels need to be substantive, relevant and accurate. Avoid repetition of labels that could cause the reader to become confused between different sections of your work.

Chapter introductions need to be carefully crafted and indicate to the reader the aims and structure of the chapter. Stylistic devices such as introductory quotations should be used with care.

Chapter conclusions need to summarize the content areas that have been covered and (in some cases) examine their implications.

Signposting needs to be used consistently throughout the thesis. Important cross-references – looking back to previous chapters or looking ahead – need to be included wherever this will tighten the overall structure.

Paragraphing also needs to be consistent throughout the thesis chapters. Check carefully for the over-organization and under-organization of text. The usual rule is one idea per paragraph.

Coherence, clarity and style checklist

This list acts as a support mechanism to enable you to review the coherence of the entire text and any sections which seem unclear or where the style of writing seems inappropriate.

Table 13.4 Coherence, clarity and style checklist

	Checked? Finalized?	*Your comments*
<u>The main point</u> of a chapter or chapter section is made clear to the reader within the introductory section		
<u>Carefully crafted topic sentences</u> help to express the main information or arguments at paragraph level		
Ideas are expressed <u>concisely</u> with all unnecessary repetition and redundancy eliminated		
Unnecessary <u>side-tracking and excessive exemplification</u> is avoided		

Unnecessarily complex sentences are avoided		
Short disconnected sentences are avoided		
The grammatical structure of sentences makes the meaning as transparent as possible		
Unnecessary imagery and exaggerated language are avoided		
Hedging language is used to qualify broad claims and assertions		
The writing style is suitably formal and adheres to conventional norms within the discipline.		

Checks here need to be at sentence, paragraph and section level, identifying in particular the following:

Redundancy: Are there any redundant words or sentences that could be cut? Are there any sections that are over-referenced that could be cut down for the sake of fluency and coherence? Are there any unnecessary digressions that could usefully be cut? Could I make more use of footnotes to help effectively manage necessary digressions? For an excellent set of guidelines for making the best use of footnotes, see Eco (2015: 167–8), who argues that there are at least eight different ways of adding information in this way.

Repetition: When repetition occurs, is it unnecessary or does it fulfil a useful purpose in highlighting important arguments? In the words of one PhD research writer, 'Sometimes I write a sentence and discover that I've already written it somewhere else'.

Complexity: Are over-complex sentences the result of problematic grammatical constructions such as the overuse of abstract nouns? Should these sentences be expressed in a simpler way? If the problem is lexical, which words will need to be substituted? According to Wolcott (1990: 52):

> Every sentence containing any form of the verb to be *is a candidate for rewriting in active voice if I can see a way to do it. Often I cannot, which makes it all the more important to improve other sentences as I am able. As I become aware of them, I also go on 'search and destroy' campaigns to ferret out overworked expressions and overused words. My current rampage is the word very.*

Hedging: Are key arguments and claims suitably hedged? Do any need to be reformulated as a result of the evidence contained in my findings?

Style: Are there any stylistic devices (such as use of 'I' or 'the researcher') that need to be modified? Are stylistic devices used consistently throughout the thesis? Have style considerations been made subordinate to the need for clarity and coherence?

Some further comments on style are worth noting. Murray (2002: 239) sensibly suggests reading your text aloud to a friend to see how the text 'sounds' in terms of its style. This is an idea that works for many writers. Remember also the wise words of Wolcott (1990: 48): 'I have never met anyone who reads qualitative studies for their style.'

Proofreading checklist

This checklist is for polishing the final version of each chapter, looking at details such as punctuation, spelling and accuracy of references.

Table 13.5 Proofreading and presentation checklist

	Checked? Finalized?	*Your comments*
Page numbers		
Accuracy of bibliographical references		
Consistency of citation style		
Cross-referencing to specific pages		
Labelling of appendices		
Labelling of diagrams and charts, numbering of tables and boxes		
Punctuation		
Spelling		
Grammatical and lexical accuracy		
Word count		
Line spacing and margins		

This is the checklist that will help you ensure that page numbers are checked, diagrams and appendices are labelled and punctuation and grammar are closely observed. The presentation format of every page of the PhD thesis needs to be closely scrutinized.

The style that you adopt in compiling your bibliography will depend on a mix of disciplinary requirements and personal preferences. There is a considerable range of styles from which to choose. *Endnote* bibliographical software now claims that it offers more than 5,000 different 'output styles'. Whatever your preferred style, you will need to check for consistency of use as well as the accuracy of your individual references.

Appendices also require careful attention. Labelling needs to be clear and consistent. The sequencing of appendix material needs to follow a logical order, usually in parallel to the development of thesis chapters. Above all, remember to check that you have included within your text *clear references to specific appendices* that will enable interested readers to explore the contextual information, extra documentation or data transcripts that have not been included in the main body of your PhD thesis. Some writers neglect this seemingly minor aspect of their work: the result is that readers are forced to discover for themselves the wealth of material that is often contained in appendices.

Finally, you have arrived at the end of a long and sometimes difficult journey. All that remains is the PhD viva.

▶ Oral presentations and writing

As a research project progresses, one very powerful way of developing and clarifying your thinking is by presenting your research orally to peers and tutors either within a disciplinary area or across disciplines. Although it might be argued that this aspect of PhD research should not be included in a handbook that focuses on writing, in fact there are strong connections between structured speaking and structured writing. Oral presentations often require the preparation of well-crafted written notes and the production of structured written handouts. The experience of presenting your research can also provide feedback that can be channelled into the writing of sections of specific chapters in the thesis.

The skills required for effective oral presentation are needed at various points of the PhD research process. Interim supervisory boards and upgrading panels may often require an oral presentation which is sometimes held in front of a larger audience. Presenting to peers at regular intervals is also expected within many disciplinary areas. Presenting at national and international conferences may take place in parallel with PhD research. Finally, there is the most significant event of all, the PhD viva.

Many researchers worry disproportionately about their oral communication skills with reference to the viva. Presenting work in progress is a useful means of allaying such fears and providing you with the self-confidence that you will need. You can also provide yourself with an opportunity to receive good quality feedback, sometimes from the most unexpected directions.

When I was studying for a PhD in the early 1990s, we were required to present our work at regular intervals as part of a series of weekly seminars. At the time, many members of academic staff within the department would come along to lend their support. We were encouraged to present to this distinguished audience, who would ask questions and would generally be polite and patient listeners. On rare occasions, they might show some irritation or incredulity. Sometimes presenters would be asked a question that really made them think. This happened to me on one memorable occasion when I was presenting my research: the question was entirely unexpected, and I did not think it was particularly relevant. I made a polite, non-committal reply, promising to think about it. Several days later when I was re-reading the draft of a chapter, the question came back to me. The more I thought about it, the more I began to realize that through a piece of interesting lateral thinking, this member of my audience had suggested another possible direction for the research. An assumption that I had inadvertently made had been questioned to great effect. I followed up the new lead that I had unexpectedly been given, and eventually it became an important strand of my research.

You can obtain great value from presenting research in progress, whatever stage you have reached. However, do not expect every experience to be comfortable or enjoyable. I have also had the negative experience of presenting some questionnaire data and having my research methodology clinically dissected by experts on survey design. As long as the experience is helpful as well as painful, we can benefit from it. If there are some inconsistencies or faults that other people perceive in our work, we should seek to know why. As discussed in the final section of Chapter 7, the important thing to remember is not to take such criticisms personally.

Criteria for effective oral presentations

Three sets of criteria relating to oral presentations are now presented for consideration. The areas that will be explored in detail are *Content*, *Structure* and *Communication Skills*. As part of the final category, there will also be a brief consideration of the interactive skills required for question-and-answer sessions that follow many structured research presentations.

Table 13.6 Oral presentation criteria checklist

CONTENT	• Too much or too little?
	• Clear or unclear aims?
	• Clear or unclear focus?
	• Interest level?
	• Originality?
	• Use of sources and referencing?

STRUCTURE and COHERENCE	• Introduction and conclusion? • Signposting? • Use of visual aids and handouts? • Main points clear? • Arguments well developed and supported? • Own standpoint clear?
COMMUNICATION SKILLS	• Empathy with audience? • Body language? (gestures, eye contact, movements) • Use of voice? (speed of delivery, highlighting of key points through word and sentence stress, intonation, pauses) • Use of speaker notes? • Presentation of all written materials? • Interactive skills when dealing with audience questions?

What makes a good oral presentation? Some speakers develop their skills intuitively, but a process of awareness raising and rationalization can help many others. Each of the three areas needs to be discussed in more detail and the most important skill areas identified.

Box 13.1. Developing Content

- Length and timing of presentation?
- Amount of material covered?
- Aims and focus of presentation?
- Relevance and interest level of topic?
- Use of source materials?

Key Skill Area 1: Include exactly the right amount of material to fit the time available. Most speakers tend to prepare too much and talk for too long, allowing only limited opportunities for questions and discussion.

Managing a strict time limit (while using the time available to maximum effect) is an important skill for a presenter. You will need to break down your research content to reveal what lies at its core. Your enthusiasm for your topic area might lead you to believe that it is shared by everyone. As a result, you may feel that an extra few minutes or a few additional examples of interesting findings cannot do anyone any harm. Resist this urge.

To help researchers manage the oral presentation of their work, initiatives such as the University of Queensland's 'Three-minute Thesis Competition' (see Appendix 1) have been devised and imitated around the world. In this type of competition a strict time limit of three minutes is imposed, while an additional constraint is added in the form of an allowance of only one single PowerPoint slide. The 'Three-minute Thesis' is popular in many countries outside Australia, since it encourages participants to develop the kind of skills that they might also need to make use of within the context of a job interview or when talking to the media.

The amount of content that you are able to cover within an oral presentation will be determined by four different factors:

- the time limit that you have been allotted – complicating factors might be very restrictive limits allowing you only a short amount of time or the need to liaise with one or more co-presenters
- your speed of delivery
- the degree of complexity of the content and your audience's ability to absorb it
- the expectations of audience members (see also Key Skill Area 3)

Box 13.2. Structure and Coherence

- Introduction and conclusion?
- Signposting of different sections?
- Use of visual aids/handouts?
- Main points made clear?
- Arguments well developed and supported?
- Own standpoint clear?

Key Skill Area 2: Organize the presentation so that information and ideas are presented in a balanced and accessible way – through a combination of spoken information, written information in handouts or PowerPoint slides and visual information in the form of pictures, charts and diagrams.

An oral presentation is a structured event in which the audience may be exposed to varying sources of input:

- the speaker's voice
- the text of PowerPoint slides
- pictures and diagrams
- audio and video recordings
- written handouts

An important skill area for any speaker involves knowing how to balance different inputs. There is little point in asking your audience to read large amounts of text while requiring that they listen to you at the same time: they will find it difficult to concentrate on both. At the other extreme, there is no need to read the content of your slides aloud, the only exception being where members of your audience are visually impaired in some way. To achieve a successful balance, it is worth considering the possible role for two important additional types of input: slides and handouts.

Slides can be of benefit to both members of the audience and speakers. They can help provide a clear structure for your talk if careful consideration is given to their sequencing and their number. One criticism of the 'Three-minute Thesis Competition' is that this benefit is removed because of the rule allowing only a single slide. In other situations, slides can provide a useful means of attracting audience attention at crucial points, thus helping to clarify and structure difficult content. This works for speakers too: you will find that you can dispense with written notes if slide selection and production have been skilfully managed.

Clearly, slides have other functions as well. They can engage and motivate audiences; can be used to add pictures, audio or video to your presentation; and can act as a useful record of the event for those who have attended your talk. Their possible disadvantages can be carefully managed. These include a tendency to 'bulletize' and over-simplify information in cases where a more in-depth analysis is required. Slides may also create a degree of audience dependency: they are now such an integral part of most academic lectures that listeners may feel lost without the structural support that they provide.

Handouts can add substantial value to oral presentations. They can supplement the oral input by providing an overview of the presentation itself or by adding more detailed descriptive information. Effective examples might include short extracts of research data, bibliographical references relating to the research, glossaries of key terms or concept definitions. All of these can be taken away to be used later by members of the audience as a record of the presentation and studied carefully. Detailed information of this type will be more difficult to convey effectively through slides.

Handouts can also contain tasks or exercises that will help provide a break during an oral presentation. However, there will be implications for time management if you stop speaking and invite audience participation in this way, so you will need to make sure that such tasks have a serious purpose. The most successful tasks will challenge audience members and seek to engage them further within your chosen topic area. A good example might be to ask them to help you analyse a few data samples.

When is the best time to distribute your handouts? Many speakers do this at the end, but this does not allow audience members to appreciate them during a talk or ask questions about them. If you talk in some detail about your data and fail to distribute the handout until you have finished speaking, this can frustrate an audience. On the other hand, you will also need to consider whether a handout given at the beginning or during a talk may prove to be an excessive distraction rather than a helpful means of support.

Box 13.3. Communication Skills

- Use of notes to aid delivery?
- Use of voice? (speed of delivery, emphasis/highlighting, intonation)
- Use of body language?
- Avoidance of redundancy and repetition?
- Pronunciation of unfamiliar words?
- Highlighting of key words?
- Suitably academic style of delivery?
- Interactive skills when dealing with audience questions?
- Rapport with audience achieved?

Key Skill Area 3: Successful communication with an audience is achieved through a combination of factors related to delivery, as well as a willingness to be flexible when executing the original plan. Presentations should never be 100 per cent prepared in advance and delivered without deviation. If no connection with the audience is established, it will be difficult for listeners to concentrate on what is being said.

The delivery of an oral presentation and the communication skills that are required to achieve an effective delivery can contribute significantly to success or failure. The key skill (which some speakers develop intuitively) is to build rapport and to empathize with your audience. Here are some questions to ask yourself:

- Am I speaking too fast or too slow?
- Do I need to pause or to repeat some information to make sure that the audience can keep pace with what I am saying?
- Are my main points being conveyed clearly and concisely to this audience?
- Why are so many people looking at their phones/at their watches/out of the window?

It is possible to develop a certain degree of paranoia when you look for audience reactions. However, the body language of your audience can act as an important source of information. Rugg and Petre (2004: 139) describe some 'classic good and classic bad signs' in this respect. Smiling and the nodding of heads can certainly act as a boost to your own self-confidence and raise your levels of enthusiasm concerning your talk – which in turn is likely to lead to more positive body language generally. There are many techniques for building rapport with an audience. The 'essential tips' section later in this chapter provides further details.

Planning research-in-progress presentations

As is the case with reader expectations for written text, it is important to take audience expectations into account when planning the structure and content of an oral presentation. Here are some elements than can merit inclusion in a 'research-in-progress' talk:

- your research topic or draft title
- your reasons for choosing this topic (and for rejecting other possibilities)
- your research questions and claims
- your research methodology and data collection methods
- influential sources: theoretical frameworks and individual writers
- your findings or expected findings
- problems encountered in the process of your research with solutions adopted

You will need to build into your planning a clear consideration of how you will present the information and achieve an effective balance between what is presented:

1. orally
2. in writing (the text of slides, handouts)
3. visually (pictures, charts, diagrams, data tables)

Dealing with audience questions

To gain maximum benefit from an oral presentation, make sure that there is sufficient time for a question-and-answer session at the end. There are some useful skill areas to develop here:

- *Anticipating likely questions so that you are prepared for them*: It is never possible or even desirable to anticipate every question. There will always be an unexpected component of each question-and-answer session. However, audiences will appreciate the fact that you have added this consideration to the planning of your presentation.

- *Clarifying what questions mean*: This is an important skill that some speakers fail to develop. Sometimes, you may feel embarrassed by your inability to understand certain questions. Long-winded contributions or multiple questions asked all together can be particularly problematic. Honesty is best in such situations. Guessing what a questioner might or might not be asking could lead to far worse embarrassment. One effective means of clarifying questions is to summarize what you have understood and to check that this is a correct interpretation. ('So what you are implying is…')
- *Dealing with questions that you cannot answer*: This is another situation where honesty is the best policy. Do not make rash promises that you will be unable to keep, such as making a firm commitment to send an answer by email the next day.
- *Knowing when to cut short the debate*: This is a final skill area that all audiences will appreciate. You may be able to deliver a long and detailed answer to a particular question: resist the temptation to do so. Cut short the debate also in situations where one questioner is beginning to dominate and where other audience members are showing signs of restlessness or irritation.

The benefits of delivering well-planned, structured oral presentations can be summarized as follows. They can:

- help you to clarify your thinking in two ways – by the very act of having to structure your thoughts and as a result of audience feedback
- act as significant milestones, providing useful deadlines within the development of your research project
- produce ideas that can feed back into writing and can suggest new avenues to explore in your reading
- become an integral part of your experience as a researcher along with upgrading interviews, conference presentations, giving lectures and the PhD viva

Box 13.4. Oral presentations: some essential tips

Content and structure of the presentation
- Plan the presentation carefully but build in some flexibility.
- Do not try to include <u>too much material</u>. Quality is paramount.
- Respect time limits; allow time for questions.

→

- State the aims of the presentation at the beginning.
- Define key terms at the beginning.
- Cut down on detail. If this is important, you can always include it in a handout.
- Have a well-defined conclusion: Do not just run out of ideas.

Delivery and communication skills

- <u>Do not read your paper</u> – this is tantamount to talking to yourself. Address your audience and be sensitive to their reactions.
- Think of different modes of delivering information: balance oral information with visual and with print (in the form of handouts).
- Make use of notes highlighting key points: Do not completely script your words.
- Be aware of body language (gestures, eye contact, facial expressions).
- Be aware of voice (intonation, volume, stress).
- Be aware of the speed of delivery.
- Draw attention to unfamiliar words: highlight if necessary in print.
- Be concise: cut out repetition and redundancy as far as possible.
- Use signposting expressions to clarify the presentation's structure.
- Listen to questions carefully and give honest answers.

▶ The viva

In the following section, the experience of the PhD viva will be considered and in particular:

- the role of the viva and its relationship to the research project
- preparing for the viva – some practical tips
- participating in the viva

The role of the viva

The *viva voce* examination marks the end of a PhD research project. According to Rugg and Petre (2004), it is a 'rite of passage' whose main purpose is to demonstrate that you have the knowledge and skills to carry out research in your chosen disciplinary area. If you are successful, you will also be considered qualified to guide other less-experienced researchers through the same process while acting as a PhD supervisor. Compared to writing a text of 80,000–100,000 words, it may appear be a relatively straightforward task. However, it represents a major obstacle for many research writers.

There are two ways of considering the PhD viva:

1. as a wonderful opportunity to celebrate the end of a successful research project, receiving the acclaim of experts within the field
2. as the last (and possibly biggest) hurdle that needs to be overcome in the race towards successful completion

The checklists in the next section suggest ways that will enable you to begin to distance yourself from position 2 and work steadily towards position 1. The viva should be an experience which is memorable for positive reasons and regarded as an opportunity rather than a threat. Too often this is not the case.

Preparing for the viva

Be prepared to wait between handing in your thesis and the viva. There may be a feeling that you are somehow relinquishing control over your work by putting it into the public domain and that it is no longer your sole property once it is out there. Think of this in a positive way – examiners are reading your work with great interest. If you can, schedule your viva at a time of day when you are most productive (see Chapter 7).

One potentially serious problem area is that after several months, you may feel differently about the text that you have written. You may have identified gaps in your text that you had not seen before. It is likely that examiners will see these too, so you should be prepared to justify them. Make sure you read your thesis through as if you were your own examiner. Read the text critically, but do not focus exclusively on what you perceive to be problem areas or deficiencies. Think of the PhD not as a definitive piece of work and an end point to a particular debate. Most examiners will tend to see it as a kind of academic exercise and as 'work in progress'.

Adding sticky notes to certain sections of the text is a useful strategy. This allows you to have evidence ready to answer questions that you have anticipated. However, be prepared for a situation where you do not need to make as much use of these as you expected. Often your perceptions of problem or weak areas in the thesis will not be matched by examiners. At the very least, your stickers will show that you have engaged with your thesis at a detailed level. And if the prospect of the viva fills you with alarm, bear in mind that there are a number of other things that you can do before the day and on the day which can be of great help. These are summarized below:

Box 13.5. Preparing for the viva

1. Think back to your upgrading/confirmation interview
Although this may seem very distant in time, it is a valuable preparation for the final viva. What kind of written comments were recorded at the time? What do you remember learning from the experience?

2. Practise the viva itself
Some supervisors are willing to organize mock vivas for research students who feel that this will be of benefit. Ideally, these should be conducted by academics who you do not know very well but who have a strong connection to your field of study.

3. Develop your oral presentation skills
Giving conference or research seminar presentations can provide an excellent preparation for the viva, enabling you to develop a range of skills, including the ability to deal with unexpected questions. They can also boost your confidence, allowing you to approach the viva with a more positive attitude.

4. Find recordings of viva interviews
These are not difficult to find. See, for example, http://www.angelproductions.co.uk/viva.htm and other recordings uploaded to YouTube.

5. Talk to PhD students who have recently undergone a viva
Talking to people who have recently undergone their viva can be very beneficial. Although experiences can differ greatly, it is useful to learn more about the type of questions that may be asked, to discover different examining styles and to be warned about possible pitfalls.

6. Anticipate the questions
These may include:

- Why did you decide to undertake this specific project?
- What are the main aims, questions and hypotheses?
- In what ways does this research make a significant contribution to your particular field of study or to related disciplinary areas?
- How do you justify your research methodology?
- What are the principal findings of this research project? How do they compare with the findings of other similar projects within the field?
- How has your thinking changed as a result of this research project?
- In hindsight, is there any aspect of the research that you would do differently?

For additional general advice on preparing for the PhD viva, go to: https://www.vitae.ac.uk/

Participating in the viva

The dynamics of a viva will change depending on the relationship between the two examiners and whether your supervisor is allowed to attend or not. A sympathetic supervisor can provide moral support even without being allowed to speak. The supervisor is also able to take detailed notes on the discussion, which can be a useful source of feedback, especially in those cases where you are required to make revisions or intend to publish your work.

During the discussions, you will find yourself in disagreement with some of the arguments presented by examiners. Be prepared to stand your ground without giving an appearance of arrogance. Strategies that will help on the day include the following:

- Listen to all questions carefully, and check that you fully understand what is expected of you. If you are not sure, do not hesitate to seek clarification.
- Answer questions clearly and concisely. If you do not know the answer, say so. Do not be tempted to digress in order to show off your knowledge on related issues – this will irritate rather than impress. Resist the temptation to deliver memorized answers.
- Stay closely connected to your written text, using specific arguments and evidence from within the thesis to strengthen the points that you make.
- Be prepared to take the initiative. If you think key points are being missed, point them out. 'Defending a thesis' does not mean adopting a purely defensive role.
- Respond to criticisms robustly if you think that they are unjustified, but have the confidence to agree if an examiner identifies a known weak area in your research. Your honesty in this respect will be appreciated.

Action Points

1. Make use of a series of checklists to help you edit first draft chapters. Check for content, structure, coherence, clarity and style.
2. Proofread the final version of all chapters carefully: check also the abstract, table of contents, bibliography and appendices.
3. Seek out opportunities to deliver 'research-in-progress' oral presentations as part of departmental seminar programmes and at conferences.
4. Plan oral presentations carefully so that you make full use of a variety of oral, visual and written inputs. Allow time for question-and-answer discussion at the end: you may gain some valuable feedback on the progress of your research.
5. Make a resolution to respect the PhD viva rather than fear it. Consider the viva as an opportunity to celebrate your work and not merely to defend it.

14 Writing throughout an Academic Career

The final chapter of this book

- considers how writing skills can be further developed beyond the production of a PhD thesis and throughout an academic career

The writing skills that you develop as an accompaniment to PhD research will be put into practice on a regular basis and gradually refined throughout your academic career. According to Blaxter, Hughes and Tight (1998: 137) such skills will be a major factor in determining career development, promotions and job satisfaction:

> *Writing is something that all academics engage in regularly: from writing notes and references on students, through committee papers, to reviews, articles and books. It is a role which many academics find hard, particularly when sustained pieces of writing are called for, but also one which can give great pleasure and a sense of achievement.*

A few years ago, I decided to explore these ideas in greater detail by collecting the testimonies of some experienced and skilled academic writers as part of a project entitled 'Writers on Writing'. I interviewed six people from a range of social science and arts and humanities disciplines. All the interviewees had an extensive list of publications: surprisingly, none had ever been asked about their views on writing or their recommendations for 'good practice'. The interview questions and the answers that I obtained are reported in a summarized version below.

What are the skills and qualities of a good academic writer?

For most people writing is something which has to be learnt and has to be developed over a long period of time. The process of writing is multi-skilled and no one is born with all of the skills that are required. It is a learning process that never stops: you can increase your skills over time if you write frequently, but it is also possible to go backwards and lose skills.

One important area is being able to make complex ideas as accessible as possible in a jargon-free way. Observing writing conventions in different contexts also requires a certain degree of skill. It is possible to be highly creative, but the right boxes still need to be ticked if writing for a specific audience, for example within a tradition such as ethnographic writing for anthropology. The balance between creativity and working within the conventions is difficult to achieve, as is the ability to weave together descriptive and more analytical writing.

There is a need to be sensitive to readers and their capacity to understand what you are saying rather than your capacity to understand it yourself. Avoid being formulaic when it comes to writing. It is better to have a portfolio of skills to select from rather than use exactly the same set of skills for each writing task.

How do experienced writers organize themselves and optimize their time?

A fixed routine would be ideal all of the time but reality often dictates otherwise, and writing has to be squeezed in wherever possible. In universities, time for writing is unfortunately rare other than in the breaks between terms when there are no teaching commitments and fewer supervisory duties. For a book with a series of deadlines, a stricter routine is usually required with well-planned break periods.

A useful aim is to try to achieve the highest level of completion (in terms of getting ideas down on paper) at the earliest possible stage. This saves time, can cut down the number of drafts and will also help you to become more skilled and self-disciplined. Another way to save time and effort is by assembling everything you need, for example notes on your reading and key quotes, so that this information is readily available to you as you write. If the writing is relatively easy (for example, referencing and footnotes), it is possible to input ideas directly onto a computer, but if more complex issues are involved, an intermediary stage such as writing in longhand will normally be required. As writing is usually seen to be the hardest part of research, you also need to ensure that you are in the best condition to undertake it. When you feel that you are in peak condition, that is when you should attempt the more demanding types of writing.

How do experienced writers obtain feedback on their writing and respond to it?

There are a number of productive ways of gaining feedback:

- Working on joint writing projects, such as co-authoring articles. Each person can provide feedback to the other, making use of their different strengths.
- Editors can help improve a written text in the case of published work. You will need to realize that they can see a text from a different perspective and are not trying to change what you are saying. Their skill is in helping you improve the way in which you communicate ideas to others.
- Friends and partners can be very useful for general feedback, in particular in helping rid writing of jargon.

There will be many situations in which writers will need to cope with negative feedback and rejection of work submitted for publication. This happens to everyone at some point. It is worth remembering that journals are refereed by people who are working under great time restraints and that the choice of referee is often arbitrary. So do not be too discouraged by rejection: this should not be allowed to knock your confidence. In the case of rejection there is usually no point in protesting: just move on and submit the article somewhere else, after having given due consideration to the feedback received.

How do experienced writers motivate themselves to write?

Even those writers who enjoy writing will usually experience a mixture of excitement and anxiety as well. Fear of not being able to fill the page is always there, no matter how much you have written. But this situation can also produce adrenalin – rather like giving a conference presentation. The first draft is always the most difficult. Once this has been completed, working with it can give lots of pleasure.

There are different experiences of writer's block, with some writers concluding that its importance has been over-exaggerated. All writers get stuck from time to time: all agree that forcing yourself to write in such circumstances is counterproductive. The usual advice is to do something different, for example a physical activity that can help to free the mind. Avoiding perfectionism also helps. Many people who get stuck with writing want to get it perfect the first time round: this can become a significant barrier to success.

What general advice can be given to less-experienced PhD student writers?

- Do not think of the thesis as 80,000 or 100,000 words to be written. Take it step by step so that it does not seem a huge task.
- It is important to have a map or outline of writing at every stage. Recognize that the map will change and that it is not set in stone.
- In the first year of PhD study, start to work on concrete chapters positioning them within the existing literature. If the work is broken up into specific chapters early on, it will be more manageable.
- Bear in mind that it is a privilege to have the time to focus on one single writing project.
- Make every effort to integrate into the research community and not become too isolated. Doing a PhD project should be fun, and life should have an element of fun. There is no evidence to suggest that those who just work are more productive.
- Stop writing only when you have an idea of how you will continue. Having to try to remember the point you reached every time you start is time consuming. So, whenever you can, finish at a point where you can start again without too much difficulty.
- Remember that writing does not come easily and involves a set of skills that are learnt over a number of years. It is possible to achieve excellence even from a seemingly hopeless starting point. But it does need to be worked upon.
- Make sure that the text is reader-friendly through the structure, the sequencing of arguments, the paragraphing and the construction of sentences. You can be too concise, or you can be too wordy: the important thing is always to ask yourself, 'who is my audience?' and 'how can I best address them?'

How important is writing as part of an academic career?

Writing is an important element of any academic career. It involves thinking ideas through and making them accessible to a wider readership. Your writing enables you to gain recognition within your field. It can also provide personal satisfaction and a significant sense of achievement. In the words of Wolcott (1990: 21):

> The conventional wisdom is that writing reflects thinking. I am drawn to a different position: writing is thinking – or stated more cautiously, writing is a form of thinking…. Writers who indulge themselves by waiting until their thoughts are 'clear' run the risk of never starting at all.

The different writing tasks that you will engage in throughout a career will have one aspect in common: your ability to write will contribute significantly to your ability to think. Writing can be seen as an ongoing learning activity: the range of writing skills that you develop as an integral part of your doctoral research are just the starting point.

A final word

Every time your written work is published and appreciated by your peers, this can act as an important career and personal landmark. When you look back on your achievement after a suitable amount of time has elapsed, you may find that you still agree with the ideas that you worked so hard to express or you may feel that you have moved on. Your writing is a record of your thinking at a particular point in your career. Successfully completing a PhD thesis is one of the most important writing achievements within this career. For this reason, I believe that it is worth looking back to see what can be learned from the whole experience through the kind of self-evaluation exercise outlined below. Once your thesis is finished, take some time to complete it, reflect on it and then pass on the results of your reflections to others who are just beginning the same journey. They will benefit from the lessons that you have learnt. In the words of one PhD writer, 'share your feelings of fear, despair, anger, frustration, disappointment, happiness, passion, encouragement, bravery and commitment'. All of these will have been present at some point, and all will have contributed to your success.

Task 14.1 Self-evaluation of the PhD writing experience

<u>Getting started</u> How difficult was it to start writing? What did you decide to write first? Was this your decision or a decision made by others? How successful were your early attempts at writing at this level?
<u>Reading routines</u> How difficult was it to manage your reading? What systems did you develop for recording your reading and notetaking? Which authors served as useful role models for your writing?
<u>Writing routines and the relationship with the reader</u> When did you manage to produce your most effective writing? How did you transform your notes into coherent text? How important was the feedback that you received from supervisors? How did you respond to negative feedback?

→

<u>Writing first draft chapters</u> How difficult was it to produce coherent first draft chapters? Which particular chapters were most problematic? Why?
<u>Maintaining motivation</u> How did you respond to occasions where you felt blocked? What were the high points and low points of writing the thesis?
<u>Editing chapters</u> How many times did you redraft and revise each of your chapters? How difficult was it to write consistently in a suitable academic style?
<u>Developing ideas</u> Did giving oral presentations help you with producing the written text? Were there any memorable events that helped you develop your text in a significant way?
<u>Causes of satisfaction and dissatisfaction</u> Which elements of your thesis have given you most cause for satisfaction? Why? Are there any aspects of your work that you would do differently in retrospect? How does this piece of writing compare with others that you have produced?

Appendix 1
Useful Websites

Chapter 1
http://www.newroutephd.ac.uk/

Chapter 2
http://the-sra.org.uk/wp-content/uploads/safety_code_of_practice.pdf
http://www3.imperial.ac.uk/secretariat/collegegovernance/provisions/
policies/scientificconduct

Chapter 3
http://www.ethos.ac.uk/

Chapter 5
http://www.collinsdictionary.com/dictionary/english
http://www.iaa.govt.nz/adviser/ethics-toolkit/personal.asp
http://www.bbc.co.uk/programmes/b00lskhg

Chapter 6
http://latex-project.org/intro.html

Chapter 7
http://sleepfoundation.org/sleep-news/backgrounder-later-school-start-
times
http://dailyroutines.typepad.com/

Chapter 9
http://www.bbk.ac.uk/mybirkbeck/get-ahead-stay-ahead
http://writersdiet.com
http://denisdutton.com/bad_writing.htm
http://www.guardian.co.uk/commentisfree/2006/dec/04/1

Chapter 10
blogs.lse.ac.uk/impactofsocialsciences/2012/11/28

Chapter 11
http://thesiswhisperer.com/2014/03/26/why-do-people-quit-the-phd/

Chapter 13
http://threeminutethesis.org/
http://www.angelproductions.co.uk/viva.htm
https://www.vitae.ac.uk/doing-research/doing-a-doctorate/completing-your-doctorate/your-viva

Appendix 2
Suggested Answers for Task 2.1

1. <u>What are the most successful marketing strategies for airline companies?</u>
   This topic is clearly too broad and possibly too descriptive in nature. Key concepts such as 'marketing strategies' and 'airline companies' seem vague and ill-defined. A significant amount of adaptation would be required to turn this into a feasible PhD research topic.

2. <u>What is the difference between management styles in Japan, the UK and the USA?</u>
   Once again, this seems overly descriptive. It may also be overly ambitious and overly complex in its attempt to compare and contrast three countries. Finally, it is unclear what would be included or excluded under the label 'management styles'.

3. <u>What are the most effective strategies for dealing with the latest generation of computer viruses?</u>
   'Most effective' suggests to the reader that there is an appropriate way of measuring the effectiveness of different strategies. Value-laden expressions of this type are not normally associated with feasible research projects. There is also the problem of defining clear boundaries for this proposed research and the added danger of the findings becoming outdated even as they are published.

4. <u>Is tourism beneficial or harmful to less developed countries?</u>
   This topic contains problematic concepts that require further definition. 'Tourism' and 'less developed countries' will need to be carefully unpacked. There is also a need for the nature of the beneficial or harmful effects to be specified: will the question be addressed from an economic, a cultural or a socio-political perspective? Or perhaps a combination of all of these?

5. <u>What are the long-term effects of sleep deprivation?</u>
   This is likely to be unsuitable for PhD research because of time constraints preventing the possibility of a longitudinal study and also because of a range of ethical considerations.

6. <u>What impact is the land reform policy in Zimbabwe having on the local economy?</u>
   There are problems inherent in studying an ongoing phenomenon. There may be further problems of data access.

7. <u>What impact will global warming have on the Maldive Islands?</u>
   The scale of this project and its predictive element are two justifiable reasons for rejecting it in its current form.

8. <u>What is the best way to improve the pronunciation of students learning English as a foreign language?</u>
   This topic aims at finding a solution to a problem which has not been defined. It also implies that there are effective ways of measuring the types of techniques that might improve the pronunciation of English language learners. It is clearly not feasible in its current form.

9. <u>Do high levels of creativity lead to psychological disturbance?</u>
   Establishing such a causal relationship would probably be beyond the scope of a PhD research project.

Appendix 3
Research Rationale Template

TITLE or TOPIC:

AIM and FOCUS OF STUDY:

CONTEXT/BACKGROUND:

RESEARCH QUESTIONS:

RESEARCH METHODS and PRIMARY REFERENCES:

ANTICIPATED FINDINGS:

References

Acocella, J. 2004, 'Blocked: Why do Writers Stop Writing?' *The New Yorker*, June 14

Andreski, S. 1971, *Social Sciences as Sorcery*, Harmondsworth: Penguin

Bauman, Z. 2003, *Liquid Love: On the Frailty of Human Bonds*, Oxford: Polity Press

Benson, P. & Voller, P. 1997, *Autonomy and Independence in Language Learning*, New York: Routledge

Billig, M. 2013, *Learn to Write Badly: How to Succeed in the Social Sciences*, Cambridge: Cambridge University Press

Blaxter, L., Hughes, C. & Tight, M. 1998, *The Academic Career Handbook*, Buckingham: Open University Press

Blaxter, L., Hughes, C. & Tight, M. 2001, *How to Research*, Buckingham: Open University Press

Booth, W., Colomb, G. & Williams, J. 1995, *The Craft of Research*, Chicago, IL: University of Chicago Press

Brewer, R. 2007, *Your PhD Thesis: How to Plan, Draft, Revise and Edit Your Thesis*, Abergele: Studymates/Baskerville Press

Bruce, N., Pope, D. & Stanistreet, D. 2008, *Quantitative Methods for Health Research*, Chichester: John Wiley & Sons

Burger, J. 2009, 'Replicating Milgram: would people still obey today?' *American Psychologist* 64(1): 1–11

Butler, J. 1999, 'A "Bad Writer" Bites Back', *New York Times*, March 20

Butler, J. 2003, 'The Values of Difficulty', in Culler, J. & Lamb, K. (eds) *Just Being Difficult: Academic Writing in the Public Arena*, Stanford, CA: Stanford University Press

Cargill, M. & O'Connor, P. 2012, *Writing Scientific Research Articles*, Oxford: Wiley Blackwell

Chomsky, N. 1965, *Aspects of the Theory of Syntax*, Cambridge, MA: MIT Press

Clark, J. 1987, *Curriculum Renewal in School Foreign Language Learning*, Oxford: Oxford University Press

Colomb, G. & Griffin, J. 2004, 'Coherence On and Off the Page: What Writers Can Know about Writing Coherently', *New Literary History* 35: 273–301

Connor, U. 2002, 'New Directions in Contrastive Rhetoric', *TESOL Quarterly* 36(4): 493–510

Cottrell, S. 2005, *Critical Thinking Skills*, Basingstoke: Palgrave Macmillan

Cresswell, J. 2003, *Research Design*, Thousand Oaks, CA: Sage Publications

Culler, J. & Lamb, K. (eds) 2003, *Just Being Difficult: Academic Writing in the Public Arena*, Stanford, CA: Stanford University Press

De Bono, E. 1970, *Lateral Thinking*, London: Penguin

Denscombe, M. 1998, *The Good Research Guide*, Maidenhead: Open University Press

Dey, I. 1993, *Qualitative Data Analysis: A User-Friendly guide for Social Scientists*, New York: Routledge

Dornyei, Z. 2007, *Research Methods in Applied Linguistics*, Oxford: Oxford University Press

Dudley-Evans, T. & St John, M., 1998, *Developments in English for Specific Purposes*, Cambridge: Cambridge University Press

Dunleavy, P. 1986, *Studying for a Degree in the Humanities and Social Sciences*, Basingstoke: Palgrave Macmillan

Dunleavy, P. 2003, *Authoring a PhD*, Basingstoke: Palgrave Macmillan

Dutton, D. 1999, 'Language Crimes: A Lesson in How Not to Write, Courtesy of the Professoriate', *The Wall Street Journal*, February 5·

Eco, U. 2015, *How to Write a Thesis*, Cambridge, MA: MIT Press

Emerson, R., Fretz, R. & Shaw, L. 1995, *Writing Ethnographic Fieldnotes*, Chicago, IL: University of Chicago Press

Enkvist, N. 1990, 'Seven Problems in the Study of Coherence and Interpretability', in Connor, U. & Johns, A. (eds) *Coherence in Writing: Research and Pedagogical Perspectives*, Alexandria, VA: TESOL

Fishman, J. 1972, *Language and nationalism; two integrative essays*, Rowley, MA: Newbury House

Frost, N. 2011, 'Writing up Pluralistic Qualitative Research' in Frost, N. (ed.), *Qualitative Research Methods in Psychology: Combining Core Approaches*, Maidenhead: Open University Press

Fulton, J., Kuit, J., Sanders, G. & Smith, P. 2013, *The Professional Doctorate*, Basingstoke: Palgrave Macmillan

Goleman, D. 1996, *Emotional Intelligence*, London: Bloomsbury

Grbich, C. 2007, *Qualitative Data Analysis: an Introduction*, London: Sage

Grix, J. & Watkins, G. 2010, *Information Skills: Finding and Using the Right Resources*, Basingstoke: Palgrave Macmillan

Hammersley, H. & Atkinson, P. 1983, *Ethnography: Principles in Practice*, London: Routledge

Hart, C. 1998, *Doing a Literature Review: Releasing the Social Science Imagination*, London: Sage

Hartley, J. 2010, 'Writing a Structured Abstract for the Thesis', *Psychology Teaching Review* 16(1): 98–100

Harwood, N. 2005, 'Nowhere has anyone attempted ... In this article I aim to do just that: a corpus-based study of self-promotional *I* and *we* in academic writing across four disciplines', *Journal of Pragmatics* 37(8): 1207–31

Hatim, B. 1997, *Communication Across Cultures: Translation Theory and Contrastive Text Linguistics*, Exeter: University of Exeter Press

Hinds, J. 1987, 'Writer versus Reader Responsibility: towards a New Typology', in Connor, U. & Kaplan, R. (eds) *Writing Across Languages: Analysis of L2 Text*, Reading, MA: Addison Publishing

Hofstede, G. 1983, 'Culture's Consequences: International Differences in Work-Related Values', *Administrative Science Quarterly* (Johnson Graduate School of Management, Cornell University) 28(4): 625–9

Holliday, A. 2002, *Doing and Writing Qualitative Research*, London: Sage

Howitt, D. and Cramer, D. 2003, *An Introduction to Statistics in Psychology*, Harlow: Pearson Education

Hyland, K. 1995, 'The Author in the Text: Hedging Scientific Writing', *Hong Kong Papers in Linguistics and Language Teaching* 18: 33–42

Levine, C. 2007, 'The Art of the Impenetrable', *Times Higher Education Supplement*, November 16

Lukas, S. 1999, 'Beyond Alphabets: An Interview with Stephen A. Tyler', *POMO Magazine* 2(1): 11–30

McCumber, J. 2003, 'The Metaphysics of Clarity and the Freedom of Meaning', in Culler, J. & Lamb, K. (eds), *Just Being Difficult: Academic Writing in the Public Arena*, Stanford, CA.: Stanford University Press

Miles, M. & Huberman, M. 1994, *Qualitative Data Analysis*, Thousand Oaks, CA: Sage

Morgan, N. 2013, *Blame my Brain: the Amazing Teenage Brain Revealed*, London: Walker

Murray, R. 2002, *How to Write a Thesis*, Maidenhead: Open University Press

Myers, D. G. 2005, 'Bad Writing', in Patai, D. & Corral, W. (eds) *Theory's Empire: An Anthology of Dissent*, New York: Columbia University Press, pp. 354–9

Nelson, V. 1993, *On Writer's Block: a New Approach to Creativity*, Boston, MA: Houghton Mifflin

Nelson, V. & Lamboll, R. 2012, *Briefing Paper: Climate Learning for African Agriculture*, Natural Resources Unit, University of Greenwich

Orwell, G. 1946, 'Politics and the English Language' in *Inside the Whale and Other Essays*, Harmondsworth: Penguin

Paltridge, B. and Starfield, S. 2007, *Thesis and Dissertation Writing in the Second Language*, Abingdon: Routledge

Patrick, P. 1998, 'Caribbean Creoles and the Speech Community', *Society for Caribbean Linguistics* XII: 1–14

Patrick, P. 2002, 'The Speech Community', in Chambers, J., Trudgill, P. & Schilling-Estes, N. (eds) *The Handbook of Language Variation and Change*, Oxford: Blackwell, pp. 573–97

Phillips, E. & Pugh, D. 2005, *How to Get a PhD: a Handbook for Students and their Supervisors*, Maidenhead: Open University Press

Ridley, D. 2008, *The Literature Review: A Step-by-Step Guide for Students*, London: Sage

Rojon, C. & Saunders, M. 2012, 'Formulating a convincing rationale for a research study', *Coaching: An International Journal of Theory, Research & Practice* 5(1): 1–7

Rugg, G. & Petre, M. 2004, *The Unwritten Rules of PhD Research*, Maidenhead: Open University Press

Said, E. 1978, *Orientalism: Western Conceptions of the Orient*, New Delhi: Penguin

Seale, C. 2004, *Researching Society and Culture*, London: Sage

Siepmann, D. 2006, 'Academic Writing and Culture: An Overview of Differences between English, French and German', *Journal des Traducteurs* 51(1): 131–50

Smart, A. 2013 *Autopilot: the Art and Science of Doing Nothing*, New York: OR Books

Sokal, A. 1996, 'Transgressing the Boundaries: Towards a Transformative Hermeneutics of Quantum Gravity', *Social Text* 46/47: 217–52

Steinbeck, E. & Wallsten, R. (eds) 1989, *Steinbeck: A Life in Letters*, New York: Penguin

Steiner, G. 1975, *After Babel: Aspects of Languages and Translation*, Oxford: Oxford University Press

Stoller, P. 1991, 'High in Fiber, Low in Content: Reflections on Postmodern Anthropology', *Culture* 11(1–2): 101–10

Swales, J. & Feak, C. 1994, *Academic Writing for Graduate Students*, Ann Arbor, MI: University of Michigan Press

Sword, H. 2012, *Stylish Academic Writing*, Cambridge, MA: Harvard University Press

Thody, A. 2006, *Writing and Presenting Research*, London: Sage

Thomas, D. 1999, *Culture, Ideology and Educational Change: The Case of English Language Teachers in Slovakia*, Unpublished PhD Thesis

Thomas, D. 2000, 'Slovakia: Language and National Unity', in O'Neill, M. & Austin, D. (eds) *Democracy and Cultural Diversity*, Oxford: Oxford University Press

Turabian, K., Booth, W., Colomb, G. & Williams, J. 2010, *Student's Guide to Writing College Papers*, Chicago, IL: Chicago University Press.

Wallace, M. 2004, *Study Skills in English*, Cambridge: Cambridge University Press

Walshaw, M. 2012, *Getting to Grips with Doctoral Research*, Basingstoke: Palgrave Macmillan

Watkins, D. & Biggs, J. (eds) 1996, *The Chinese Learners: Cultural, Psychological and Contextual Influences*, Melbourne and Hong Kong: ACER & CERC

Wierzbicka, A. 1997, *Understanding Cultures Through Their Key Words*, Oxford: Oxford University Press

Williams, J. 1995, *Style: Toward Clarity and Grace*, Chicago, IL: University of Chicago Press

Williams, R. 1976, *Keywords*, London: Fontana

Willis, R. & Cowton, C. 2011, 'Looks Good on Paper', *Times Higher Education Supplement*, August 4

Wisker, G. 2005, *The Good Supervisor*, Basingstoke: Palgrave Macmillan

Wolcott, H. 1990, *Writing up Qualitative Research*, Newbury Park, CA: Sage

Yin, R. 1994, *Case Study Research: Design and Methods*, Thousand Oaks, CA: Sage

Zerubavel, E. 1999, *The Clockwork Muse: A Practical Guide to Writing Theses, Dissertations and Books*, Cambridge, MA: Harvard University Press

Index